THE RESILIENCE DRIVE

100 simple practices to navigate daily challenges with joy and success

Translated into English by Paula Cook

Favre S.A. Editions
Head office: 29, rue de Bourg- CH- 1002 Lausanne
Tel: (+41) 021 312 1717 Fax: (+41) 021 320 50 59
lausanne@editionsfavre.com

Paris office:
7, rue des Canettes - F - 75006 Paris

www.editionsfavre.com

Legal deposit in Switzerland on October 2017 for the original edition in French under the title *L'élan de la résilience*.

Illustrations: Jenay Costantini - Loetscher

Layout and graphic design: Dynamic 19

ISBN: 978-2-8289-1704-3

Favre Editions benefit from a structural support by Office fédéral de la culture for years 2016-2020

Alexia Michiels

THE RESILIENCE DRIVE

100 simple practices to navigate daily challenges with joy and success

FAVRE

To the love of my life, Benoit.

To our children, Victoria, Zoé, Ari and Eva:
May you live all your dreams consciously.

TABLE OF CONTENTS

STIMULATE YOUR VITALITY

ENGAGE YOUR EMOTIONS

TRAIN THE MIND

SPIRIT IN ACTION

FOREWORD

Today's crises and urgencies, extensively relayed by the media, incite more fear and confusion than hope and energy. Beyond societal preoccupations, you are also facing the challenges of everyday life - whether simple or complex. Your agenda is overbooked, your lifestyle is hectic, your work leaves little time for other priorities; your energy level is often low and you rarely take time to settle down... Does this ring a bell?

Resilience is essential to juggle family life and professional ambition, to honour your commitments without being exhausted, or more so, to radiate and blossom, every day. Resilience is nurtured day after day, inviting us to rally and align all of our resources - body, heart, mind and spirit - to navigate serenely the uncertain seas of today's complex world.

This book is an invitation to consciously take charge of your life and to enjoy the freedom of choice! You are invited to choose from a range of simple and tested practices. Select those you find the most useful, accessible and balanced considering your personal situation and affinities.

Practical approach

Recognising the interest of a concept is not enough. An interesting idea that is not translated into a behaviour has very little influence. To give the impulse of change and begin a genuine transformation, consciousness must translate into behavioural change. Everyday life – encompassing all your habits – conditions your capacity to successfully face challenges and flourish.

It starts by taking responsibility for yourself. How will you honour your responsibilities without draining your energy? How will you reach high objectives whilst radiating? How can you live abiding by your personal values? This book suggests some answers to these questions through 100 simple practices that will inspire you to create a daily routine that serves you. For the most pragmatic amongst you, scientific evidence supports the practices and punctuates your reading.

Since nothing is as true as the echo of those who have experienced resilient practices, I have also compiled some testimonials of men and women who decided to actively strengthen their resilience and experienced THE RESILIENCE DRIVE. I hope that you will find in this book the motivation to initiate your own journey and remember: every single step in the right direction is a step towards transformation.

"A journey of a thousand miles begins with a single step."

Laozi.

PREFACE
By Doctor Sven Hansen, Founder of The Resilience Institute

I am delighted and honoured to share this preface for Alexia's new book. Alexia is the third published practitioner in our team. This is a wonderful addition to our work and resources. I am confident this guide will help many people in practical ways.

The idea of Resilience took a while to develop. Coming from a medical family with a strong sports background and two years in the army in South Africa in Special Forces[1], medicine was a shock. In fact, I became quite depressed at the futility of desperately patching up symptoms whether through major surgery or medication. It was clear that patients would go back to the same lives and habits that got them sick in the first place.

Inspired by my father's work on the prevention of nutritional problems in children, I found my mission in my final year. Why not apply the wonderful science of medicine and biology to keep people well and out of hospital whenever possible? That is exactly what I did in my first clinic in Christchurch in 1988. My colleagues thought I was deranged.

---

1 Special Forces, as defined by NATO, are military units trained to conduct special operations.

We faced massive obstacles. Why would someone pay for prevention if the hospital system was free or insurers picked up the bill? It was a huge challenge to find and develop clients who were interested in investing in their well-being. The medical profession actively resisted our work.

Over the next 10 years the concept matured into the Resilience Institute. It was clear that sustainable well-being had physical, emotional and mental elements. Through the 1990s we built up our approach and solutions to include mastering stress, emotional intelligence and training the mind. Business started to take notice.

The 21st century changed the game. Suddenly people realised the power and cost benefit of prevention and well-being investments. The cost of our fast-paced lives and distress was measurable. Good leaders and professionals needed to build emotional intelligence and learn how to train their minds to address the complexity. Leading businesses started to seek us out. Our work expanded from New Zealand, into Australia and on to Asia where I met Alexia.

In 2017, it is a whole new world. Our volatile, uncertain, complex and ambiguous (VUCA) world has made Resilience a core competence for leaders, professionals and workers to survive and thrive. The ability to demonstrate rapid bounce, courage, connection and creativity (our definition of Resilience) can clearly be learned and has massive economic benefits.

Preventative medicine, positive psychology, sports science and neurobiology have boomed with thousands of papers per week investigating the different aspects of resilience - physical, emotional, cognitive and even spiritual. Thankfully, our various hypotheses and methodologies now have massive peer-reviewed support.

Today's challenge is to keep our material up to date with new evidence. More importantly, we strive to communicate in practical and meaningful ways. Often, we know too much and do too little. While cutting edge brain science is exciting, the simple disciplines of sleeping, eating and exercising well, mastering distress, cultivating emotional wisdom, and the will to focus enable the brain and a good life.

It is in these practical elements that Alexia's work excels.

Meeting Alexia was meant to be. Both my wife and I had been working independently in Shanghai back in 2009. While negotiating an opportunity in China, my wife returned from Shanghai clutching the daily paper. In it was a full spread on this impressive coach who was taking an integral and holistic approach to coaching. The article was on Alexia.

Thus began a wonderfully creative and productive relationship with Alexia. We worked together on projects in China culminating in her training as a practitioner with us back in 2009. Alexia and her family then moved back to Europe and co-founded The Resilience Institute Europe. Since then, she has supported thousands of executives to enrich their lives and leadership.

Alexia walks the talk. Mother in a dynamic family, she effortlessly practices and teaches yoga, completes marathons, skis, and trains demanding executives. She has truly found a way to integrate physical, emotional, cognitive and spiritual development. We are very blessed to have her on our team. Her book will help to understand and diffuse the benefits of resilient practices.

When Alexia announced that she was going to write a guide, I had no doubt it would be a valuable contribution to many lives. Writing is testing. Few complete the task. How Alexia has achieved this in her busy life is remarkable. So, when Alexia offers to share 100 simple practices to build resilience, you can be sure that these have been tested and have delivered positive results.

Be curious, select the practices that get your attention, practice hard and enjoy the benefits.

PREFACE
By Dr Joël de Rosnay, Scientist and Writer

Personal growth through mastering resilience

The concept of resilience leads to two complementary approaches: a dynamic approach and a permanent condition that supports physical and spiritual equilibrium. Alexia Michiels intelligently and pertinently progresses between these dynamic and permanent approaches: "Resilience is nurtured day after day, inviting us to rally and align all our resources - body, heart, mind and spirit - to navigate serenely the uncertain seas of today's complex world".

This culture of resilience, this way of managing body and mind is very similar to a principle to manage one's life that I call bionomics. To understand the scope of this idea, we must draw a parallel between ecology and economics. Ecology is the science (logos) of the home (oikos), whereas economics is the management rules (nomos) of this home. In fact these are two sides of the same coin. I realised that although biology existed (bio-logos, the science of the living), there was no such thing as bio-nomos, or bionomics: the principle of managing one's life. Being bionomical suggests using one's body and life with care, knowing how to look after oneself and managing oneself responsibly. In fact, we teach our children to be economical, not bionomical. Being bionomical means applying very simple principles to manage one's health capital, life capital and mental capital. It means being continuously resilient. Those who do not apply the rules of resilience, so well described in this book, spend their lives trying to manage time and information simultaneously. The problem is that we never have enough time to do what we would like to, but we have far too much information. The impossibility to manage time and information in a balanced way leads to feeling "overwhelmed" or "not to have enough time". This flawed life management and ensuing unbalance lead to what we call "burnout", an incapacity to act efficiently that can have severe psychological consequences and precipitates a syndrome of exhaustion or depressive state. The Human Resources Directors of companies are well acquainted with such difficult situations. Hence the importance of including when managing human capital.

Alexia Michiels gets it right and focuses her book on stress mastery and life balance. Resilience is a multifaceted concept that involves physical, emotional, cognitive and spiritual factors. This set of skills allows cultivating energy, managing stress, connecting positively to oneself and others and finding meaning. In this sense, it matches the modern approaches of epigenetics (the modulation of the expression of the genes through behaviours). Resilience must be considered as the priority of personal epigenetics to contribute to manage ageing optimally. This management represents an art, a science and a technique. I like the English expression for successful ageing: successful maturing. In the face of old age, we can no longer think in terms of causes and effects, in analytical terms. It is crucial to understand that the three main networks of the body - nerves, immunity and hormones - constantly communicate between themselves. In biology, everything is connected, and ageing cannot be associated with one specific cause.

Resilience also perfectly applies to a sport I know well: surfing. One must have willpower and resistance to dare confronting these huge waves. One must sometimes stay on board for long periods of time without catching one's breath, staying in an "uncontrolled balance" on the board and the wave... a basic principle for the resilience of surfers. I have applied these principles to life in my book Surfer la vie. Life is a wave that you can surf with joy and purpose through resilience.

I find many common points with Alexia Michiels' propositions in her beautiful book, which works as a management code for the body and mind through physical and mental resilience. When you are resilient, you feel good about yourself and live to give and radiate. Resilience inspires and helps to flourish. I shall conclude with the words of Alexia Michiels: "The competencies that allow bouncing back in adverse situations by calling upon all our resources are similar to those competencies leading to fulfilment". Truly a beautiful life lesson.

INTRODUCTION

My personal journey did not immediately lead me to resilience. I was raised in a large family in Belgium and enjoyed a traditional and happy youth without major dramas. After graduating with a Bachelor in Economic and Consular Sciences (at Brussels' ICHEC), I worked for ten years in the marketing and media world (Procter & Gamble, RTL TVi, World Federation of Advertisers). I married young and became a young mother... Curious and eager to discover more about the world, my husband and I were ready to flee the nest and see the world. We lived in China, in Shanghai for five fascinating and decisive years...

Confronted with a drastically different culture from what I then perceived as "the norm", I took advantage of this experience to de-condition myself - a little bit - in order to better know myself and reconnect with my own values. This led me to start training as a certified professional coach (ICA - International Coach Academy). I also practised yoga so much that I decided to start teaching it and obtained my certification (Inspya Yoga). As its name indicates, this discipline (yoga = union) progressively led me to understand and feel that I was more than my thoughts. I was a "whole" emerging from the various dimensions that were part of me (body, heart, mind and spirit). By consciously mobilising these dimensions, I could create serenity and harmony.

In 2008, I met Dr Sven Hansen - Founder of the Resilience Institute - who was lecturing in Shanghai. My husband Benoit Greindl had invited him to facilitate a workshop for Chinese and expat entrepreneurs. Everyone was hooked and moved by Sven's holistic and pragmatic approach. Sven understood that resilience must be nurtured every day, not simply to bounce back quicker in the face of life's challenges, but also to live every day fully. Sven's pragmatic approach is influenced by his medical background and enables him to broach subtle topics using a practical and rational language. I was convinced!

By joining the Resilience Institute, I would be able to approach the workplace and I would contribute to putting men and women back at the heart of the organisations' preoccupations. This condition is crucial to achieve sustainable performance and progressively build a better world.

This book stems from ten years spent coaching and training managerial teams. It also - and perhaps particularly - reflects a practice that I progressively integrated to my own life, with benefits that I enjoy every day.

I am deeply grateful to Dr Sven Hansen for showing me this path and to my partners at the Resilience Institute for the immense joy of experiencing this adventure together.

What exactly is resilience?

Physics offers the original definition of the word. It relates to the mechanical characteristics that define a material's resistance to shocks. Psychologists including French Boris Cyrulnik often use this image to allude to the capacity to bounce back in the face of adversity or to overcome traumatic situations.

Since then, the concept of resilience has evolved. It encompasses a range of skills enabling to bounce back when facing adversity but also to lead a successful and fulfilling life - both personally and professionally.

Resilient people demonstrate rapid bounce, courage and creativity; they cultivate healthy connections with themselves, others and the environment.

Why daily resilience?

As time goes by, the work pace accelerates. Productivity expectations increase; technology subjects you to the necessity or temptation to stay virtually (and continuously) connected to your family, friends and colleagues, but also to the world in general since information flows endlessly.

Today´s lifestyles combine professional demands and the ambition of "living a fulfilling personal life" leading to numerous cases of burnout and exhaustion. People run like headless chickens from one meeting to the next, from one deadline to the next, from one project to the next... There is little time left for reflection in this rat race. Everything goes too fast, and your mind is overwhelmed with information.

Epigenetics or the impact of habits

What influences resilience? Genes or the environment? Is it innate or learned? While some individuals boast a deterministic vision and believe that resilience competencies are innate and inalterable, others observe how resilience evolves with the environment, life experiences, practices and the will to progress. I am of the latter category, with a more optimistic and constructive vision of resilience. The recent emergence of epigenetics tends to prove us right!

Genetics is a branch of biology studying genes. Genes make up a mere 2% of our DNA, known as "coding DNA", which defines us as we are - our gender, eye colour, hair colour... but what about the remaining 98% of DNA? Since it is not made up of genes, scientists thought it useless and named it "junk DNA". Recent research now suggests that this high percentage of so-called junk DNA is directly responsible for the expression - or non-expression - of our genes (2% of coding DNA).

This discovery led to a new fascinating and revolutionary field of research: epigenetics, i.e., the study of the modification of gene expression depending on our environment, lifestyle and habits. Obviously, some people seem to be "naturally" better equipped than others to bounce back in the face of adversity and to show resilience in their everyday life. Epigenetics demonstrates that genetic predispositions alone or the environment on its own do not characterise someone; but the interaction between both does.

This opens the door to a wide range of possibilities: your daily habits and present actions can influence your future "you", your health and your resilience!

Resilience at work

The World Economic Forum attests that we have entered the 4th industrial revolution. After mechanisation, electrification, and automation, we now live in the digitalisation era. Robots and Artificial Intelligence quickly progress and invade every part of our life. The work environment is seriously impacted, since robots will soon execute many tasks accomplished by humans - and many already do! Researchers at Oxford University estimate that 47% of American jobs will be automated 20 years from now.

This finding is simultaneously frightening and exciting. Here is a unique opportunity to reconnect with your deepest human resources and to value and cultivate your intrapersonal and interpersonal skills that set you apart from machines.

Resilience defines a set of skills that you can learn and strengthen. Being calm, physically energised, in touch with your emotions and those of others, mentally clear and spiritually guided by values giving meaning to your action.

Values and ethics become increasingly essential in a digital world. What choices are to be made? What programming criteria are to be applied? We cannot decently leave these questions to chance...

The resilience spiral

Founded by Dr Sven Hansen in 2002, the Resilience Institute offers a simple model to become conscious of the interaction between the various dimensions that make up an individual (body, heart, mind, spirit) and to reinforce your flexibility - the ability to navigate through life´s stormy waters and peaceful seas - with more ease and serenity. This is known as "the resilience spiral".

In a world where we tend to constantly rush forward, the resilience spiral invites to take on a more vertical perspective of life.

Stop for a minute. Think about what is essential to you; what drives you, what inspires you... At the same time, reflect on your current state. Where are you on the spiral?

After more than 400 years´ influence on our education and vision of the world, Descartes and his adage: "I think therefore I am" are fundamentally challenged. Recent research in the areas of neuroscience, positive psychology or biology allow reintegrating into our life some ancient wisdom principles that consider the individual as a whole, not only as a walking brain! Using recent scientific learning, we can now address these themes very pragmatically.

The following pages offer you to experiment - simple and tested - resilient practices classified in five chapters that will take you on an inspiring journey through the resilience spiral. Chapter VI, before the conclusion, invites you to take action today. You will be encouraged by the testimonials of people who started a resilience journey and accepted to share the benefits they experienced.

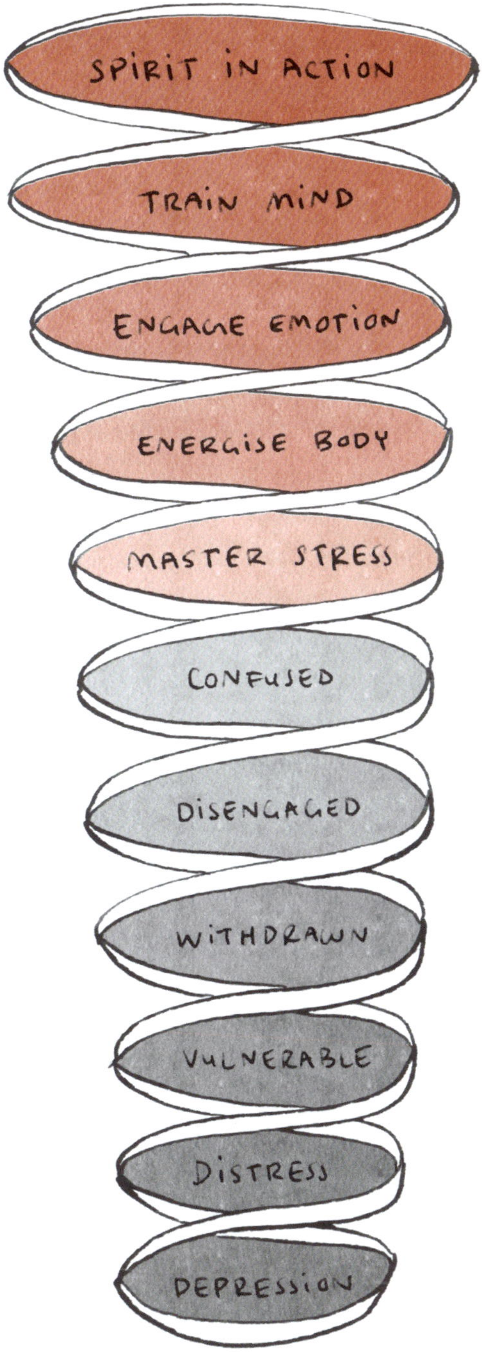

SPIRIT IN ACTION

TRAIN MIND

ENGAGE EMOTION

ENERGISE BODY

MASTER STRESS

CONFUSED

DISENGAGED

WITHDRAWN

VULNERABLE

DISTRESS

DEPRESSION

CHAPTER I

STAY CALM AND REJUVENATE

Practice #1 - Cultivate awareness

Take a moment today to pinpoint your position on the resilience spiral.

Take a step back and look at yourself. You will develop awareness, learn to know yourself better and reinforce your personal resilience.

Research demonstrates the benefits of self-awareness for success and well-being. In an article published in Perspectives on Psychological Science[1], scientist Mary Helen Immordino-Yang suggests that personal reflection is key to understand oneself and manage one's life in the outside world.

Korn Ferry[2] research also demonstrated the direct link between the self-awareness of leaders and financial health of an organisation. In their article "A better return on self-awareness", Zes and Landis write that companies listed on the stock

1 MH. Immordino-Yang et al., "Rest Is Not Idleness: Implications of the Brain's Default Mode for Human Development and Education", Perspectives on Psychological Science, 2012.

2 D. Zes, D. Landis, "A better return on self-awareness", Korn Ferry Institute, 2013.

exchange with a higher "return on investment" also hire professionals who demonstrate a higher self-awareness.

What's your altitude on the resilience spiral today?

Practice #2 - Exhale and remain calm under pressure

Today, grasp every opportunity that you can to breathe out slowly and remain calm under pressure.

By breathing out, you activate the brain's parasympathetic system, which controls relaxation. Whilst you lead an intense and busy life, the ability to remain calm under pressure could explain the crucial difference between success and failure. Remaining calm under pressure means that you are less likely to suffer the effects of stress, anxiety and worries. Cultivating calm also leads to better health and a higher productivity rate. Moreover, it improves your communication, helping you make better decisions.

Who will benefit from your calm today?

Follow the guide

- Settle down comfortably on a chair, back straight, shoulders loosened.
- Breathe in through the nose and count to 4: 1, 2, 3, 4
- Breathe out through the mouth and count down from 6 to 1: 6, 5, 4, 3, 2, 1
- Repeat 3 times.

By concentrating a moment on your breathing, you are calming the mind. By exhaling lengthily, you are experiencing real time relaxation. Slower breathing calms your physiology and regulates your heartbeat. When your heart beats regularly, we speak of "cardiac coherence". Cardiac coherence champions the ideal oxygenation of the brain. Regular heartbeats send regular signals to the brain, which then functions optimally.

Conversely, an irregular heartbeat (such as when you are feeling overwhelmed or threatened by a unexpected question) sends irregular signals to the brain, which can limit your cognitive ability. This is what can happen to students during oral examinations. When standing in front of a teacher asking a question , which the student cannot answer, the student's cognitive abilities are diminished by poorly managed pressure.

Practice #3 - Do a spinal twist

Today, take advantage of short breaks throughout the day by doing regular spinal twists.

Working statically for long hours provokes tensions in the spine and upper back. You may not realise this, but you move a little less when you are under stress. Vertebrae become compressed and tensions appear. It's the right moment to do a spinal twist. Be careful to do the twist on each side.

The torsion liberates the body from physical tensions and provides a pleasant moment of relaxation.

Why not dispel all your back tensions?

Practice #4 - Close your eyes

Throughout the day, close your eyes for a few seconds to practice instantaneous relaxation.

Most tasks are completed in front of a computer screen and engender a sensation of tiredness. For immediate relaxation, close your eyes for a few seconds and loosen all facial muscles, particularly around the eyes.

A scientific study by the University of Surrey[3] even indicates that closing one´s eyes opens up intelligence!

How about closing your eyes... here and now?

Practice #5 - Take a micro-break

Today, treat yourself to regular micro-breaks during your working day.

A micro-break lasts from 30 seconds to 5 minutes and allows your body to release the accumulated tensions, thus reducing risks of pain linked to long periods of time spent in front of a computer. This helps fight fatigue and boasts a positive effect on productivity, problem solving and creativity.

Did you know that working more than 50 minutes uninterruptedly leads to - difficultly perceptive, albeit real - decreased attention?

Studies[4] have demonstrated that a micro-break every 40-45 minutes could help avoid this loss of attention.

When will you take your next micro-break?

---

3 University of Surrey. Journal Legal and Criminal Psychology. 2015.

4 R. A. Henning, S. L. Sauter, G. Salvendy and E. F. Krieg, "Micro break Length, Performance, and Stress in a Data Entry Task", Ergonomics, 1989.

Follow the guide

There are many forms of micro-breaks. Consciously interrupt what you are doing for 30 seconds to 5 minutes. Here are some examples of efficient micro-breaks:

- Get up and get a glass of water;
- Roll back your shoulders 3 times in a row;
- Look at the scenery through the window;
- Offer your colleague a cup of tea/coffee;
- Pay attention to your breathing (see practice #2) and focus on exhalation.

Practice #6 - Go to another room

If you feel the pressure rising today, go to another room!

Changing room is sometimes enough to take some distance from a tense situation or when the pressure becomes too high. Creating space between oneself and a situation (or a person) at home or at work often helps you rejuvenate and calm down.

How about (literally) taking some distance?

Practice #7 - Visualise calm

Today, spend a little time to visualise calm.

Visualisation consists of imagining yourself in a peaceful place by mentally connecting yourself to what you /hear/feel or sense when you are in that exact location. Science shows that visualisation boasts immediate physiological well-being, slows down the heartbeat and triggers a feeling of relaxation.

What calm place will you visualize today?

What if this were you?

Bernard teaches math to young people aged between 15 and 17. He loves his job and shares his passion with his pupils. For some time, he has noted that the level of concentration diminishes: a few inattentive teenagers agitate the group and this has an adverse effect on the concentration needed to assimilate the course matter. Bernard is nervous before even starting to teach. His authority wanes and his level of tolerance decreases.

He decides to work on his inner calm to stimulate serenity amongst his students. Before going into the classroom, Bernard takes a moment to visualise the country house where he spends his weekends. For one minute, he connects to what he feels when he is there. He creates calm.

He feels serene and can start teaching in better "inner" conditions. He observes that the agitation in the class decreases when he is feeling calm and relaxed.

Visualisation refers to the mental capacity of representing a situation, person or sensation. Depending on its intensity, this mental representation can trigger approximately the same physiological effects than that of reality. Through a visualisation exercise, Bernard builds a detailed image of the place that inspires and calms him. When the exercise is done with a high level of attention, the emotions felt are similar to those felt more intensely in real situations. These positive emotions tend to bring Bernard to a state of relaxation. He is then better prepared to start giving his lessons.

Practice #8 - Set aside some "me time"

Today, check your agenda and set aside some "me time" in the coming week.

Taking some "me time" provides both psychological and physical benefits. When taking a break to do something that you like, you feel more awake and happier. Concentrating on an activity that you are practicing just for you decreases stress levels and recharges your batteries.

When will you take some "me time" this week?

Practice #9 - Relax your face

Today, take some time to relax your facial muscles.

When days are long and busy, your face reflects the internal physical or emotional tension that you feel. By consciously loosening the facial muscles, particularly around the eyes, you are in fact practising a form of short - albeit efficient - self-relaxation.

How do you feel when your face is relaxed?

Follow the guide

If you are feeling tired or particularly tense, this simple routine will help loosen the muscles around your eyes.

- Rub your palms together and bring your hands close to your face without touching it. Your eyes are shut, and you can feel the heat generated from the palms.
- Using your forefinger and middle finger, lightly press the space between your eyes (sometimes called the "third eye") upwards. Repeat 5 times.

- Then, using your clenched fist, draw an 8 figure around the eyes, going over the nose. Repeat 10 times.

This exercise energises the eyes and activates the microcirculation around them, helping reduce bags under the eyes whilst reinforcing the eyelids.

Practice #10 - Write down your worries

Today, write down your worries in a notebook.

The act of writing inspires you to use the right words. Formulating clearly preoccupations helps create more clarity and coherence. A study of the University of Chicago[5] demonstrated that writing about one's worries has a calming effect and tends to decrease the intensity of stressful thoughts.

Which words accurately describe your current worries?

Practice #11 - Take the child's pose

Today, at the end of your day, take a child's pose for 2 minutes.

"Balasana" is the Sanskrit word that defines the child's yoga pose. This posture is particularly efficient to relieve backache whilst increasing blood flow, stretching the thigh muscles and decreasing tiredness. By placing your arms along your body, palms turned upwards, you are relaxing the upper back muscles and shoulders.

Are you ready to loosen your shoulders and relax your back?

---

5 University of Chicago, "Writing about testing worries boosts exam performance in the classroom", Journal Science, 2011.

Practice #12 - Relativise and project yourself in the future

Today, use the projection technique to relativise a situation.

When things don't go as you wish, think about projecting yourself into the future and ask yourself this question: "Will this still be important one year from now?" You'll be surprised to see that, nine times out of ten, the answer is no and will allow you to easily chase away recurrent negative thoughts.

Will this still be important one year from now?

Practice #13 - Reconnect with nature

Today, take an opportunity to reconnect with nature.

Reconnecting with nature is an invitation to rediscover your true self. After a walk, time spent outdoors or practising a sport outside, you are reconnecting with a natural environment that is all too often lacking from our cities.

Humans have evolved in close connection with nature and 300 years of industrialisation cannot deny this key aspect of evolution. Ancient civilisations, Chinese, Greek and Roman, were all convinced that spending time outdoors was healthy. After years of research, we know today that their intuition was right.

What if this were you?

Pierre is a young, single man with no children. He is self-employed in a start-up in the food industry. Pierre is passionate about his work and resolute to reach his goals. He works diligently and makes no real distinction between weekdays and weekends. He does feel some fatigue, but this does not trouble him since he loves his job!

One day, one of his friends invites him for a weekend away in the mountains. Hesitant at first, he eventually agrees. He spends a regenerative weekend and feels invigorated when he returns. The next week goes smoothly and Pierre makes headway on many projects.

Pierre then realises just how beneficial his connection to Nature was, even feeding his creativity. From then on, he decides to set aside some time to spend in nature several times a week, ranging from long walks to shorter strolls when he pops out of the office to go around the local park.

Several studies have demonstrated the benefits of nature on men and women. A study published by British association Ramblers and MacMillan Cancer Support[6] showed that 2 1/2 hours walking or gardening every week contribute to fighting anxiety and creates more well being.

6 D. de Moor, "Walking Works", Rambler and MacMillan Cancer Support Report, 2013.

David Strayer[7], a professor in neurosciences at the University of Utah demonstrated that spending time immersed in a natural environment leads to a measurable and significant advantage for creativity. By being aware of the benefits of his weekend in the mountains, Pierre played with his agenda to integrate moments of reconnection with Nature. He enjoys the positive influence of the latter on his well-being and creativity.

Practice #14 - Be grounded

Today, take some time to ground yourself.

Grounding oneself consists of - simply albeit consciously - pressing one's feet flat on the ground whilst standing upright, arms along the body. Feet spread hip-width apart for stability. The simple action of grounding reinforces presence and self-confidence, which is particularly important in difficult moments.

When possible (and this is not necessarily the case in a professional setting!), practise this exercise bare-footed. The grounding technique on bare feet gives a sensation of rooting, and some people go as far as to say that the earth's energy can chase away the negative energy accumulated in our bodies. In the same way as the contact between the earth and electrical equipment drains the latter without danger, the same phenomenon is said to take place once one is grounded, bare feet on the ground. Your electric frequency balances out and harmonises with that of the Earth.

How about standing up and pressing your feet to the ground?

7 Strayer and Atchley, "Creative in the Wild", Plos One journal, 2012.

Practice #15 - Listen to your body

Today, pay attention to the signals that your body sends.

Your physiology is constantly searching for optimal balance and repetitively activates various physiological changes to reach this ideal point. This phenomenon is called homoeostasis, a regulation process by which the body tends towards equilibrium.

Although this is not generally visible from the outside, the functioning of your body is subject to a biological rhythm of 24 hours. We speak of "chrono-biology". Production of hormones, heart rate, blood pressure, skin regeneration, fatigue or growth are some of the many factors that change throughout the day and that depend on the external environment and activities, emotions and thoughts. By listening to your body, you learn to better know and respect yourself. The signals sent by your body are warnings that may become more painful if ignored for too long!

What does your body tell you today?

Follow the guide

To listen to your body, take a moment and stop what you are doing. Pay attention to your inner self and ask yourself the following questions:

- What is my current energy level?
- Am I tired?
- Am I physically tense or relaxed?
- Am I hungry or thirsty?
- Do I feel pain somewhere?

Practice #16 - Walk slower

Today, take some time to walk slower and slacken your pace.

Your days are filled with back-to-back meetings, deadlines, timetables and jobs. At home or at work, you are like most of us, always on the run! Slackening the pace allows to - physiologically - slow down your heart rate by adopting a slower rhythm and to rejuvenate in the here and now rather than running after the next minute. Slowing down is a strategy that could ultimately help you save time!

What will you experience by walking slower?

Practice #17 - Disconnect from screens

Today, why don't you put aside some time from screens and enjoy a "pause" before reconnecting?

The term "screen" includes tablets, smartphones and computers. New technologies have created new dependencies. By limiting screen time, you are effectively encouraging "genuine" relationships and limiting the negative effects of screens on your health - particularly on the quality of sleep! Research indicates that more than 60% of the population spends up to 4 hours every day in front of a screen, 5 hours for children! How long do you spend in front of your screen each day?

A study carried out in 2013 by Ifop[8] showed that 40% of users are incapable of spending an hour without checking their phone while 78% of youth aged under 25 is addicted to smart phones. So-called "behavioural" addictions to screens

8 IFOP, "Les Français et la dépendance au téléphone portable", 2013 (the French and their mobile phones).

are starting to emerge, with effects comparable to games addiction, compulsive buying disorder or sexual addiction. If you check your emails first thing in the morning, if you log on to your social networks before falling asleep or if you cannot stay away from your smartphone without feeling depressed, this practice will prove tremendously positive.

Who will benefit the most from no-screen time?

What if this were you?

Marco is 43 years old. He is married and has two children. Marco works for an insurance company and goes from meeting to meeting during the day. He has no time to deal with all the incoming messages and spends a good part of his evening answering requests. When his children are asleep, he starts working again. Exhausted, Marco falls asleep easily but wakes up at around 4am, unable to go back to sleep... He sleeps too little and is accumulating a heavy sleep-debt.

Marco has decided to take matters into his own hands and to experiment with a resilient practice: he stops checking his messages at 8:30pm. Astonished by the immediate impact of this new routine, he no longer wakes up at 4am but at 6am, after a good night's rest. From 5 hours, he is up to 7 hours slumber each night. He feels more rested, serene and efficient during the day.

A good night is anything between 7 to 8 hours of uninterrupted sleep and the quality of sleep depends on what you are focusing on just before bed. By checking his email on his mobile phone, Marco suffers a twofold negative effect: blue light exposure (from his smartphone) stimulates the brain and additional information that represents so many stimuli, encouraging the brain to stay alert.

To enjoy a restorative night, your brain must progressively go into sleep mode. Allow at least one hour with no exposure to screens to best prepare for a good night's sleep!

Practice #18 - Listen to relaxing music

Today, cultivate calm by listening to relaxing music for 3 minutes.

Research[9] demonstrates that listening to relaxing music decreases the heart rate, lessening blood pressure and increasing serotonin levels (the "neurotransmitter of happiness") and other hormones with beneficial effects on the bloodstream.

Relaxing music allows an escape from daily pressure, improves the quality of sleep and develops learning capacities.

Do you have some relaxing music on your playlist?

Practice #19 - Do a body scan

Today, take a few minutes to do a body scan.

Lying on your back, be your own guide. Focus your attention on each part of your body, scanning the latter from toes to head. Although this technique is very simple, it allows reconnecting with your body, relax physical tensions and calm down an agitated mind. This technique is also very effective to reinforce attention control. Who can deny that lying on one's back and reconnecting to one's body - without any form of judgment - can be anything but positive?

What perfect moment will you choose to do your body scan today?

---

9 Harvard Medical School, "How music can help you heal", 2016.

Follow the guide

To do a body scan, go to a quiet place and lie down or sit comfortably.

- Close your eyes and start by paying attention to your breath.
- Stay focused on what you are physically feeling.
- Focus your attention on your feet and ankles.
- Feel your shins and calf muscles.
- Focus your attention on each knee.
- Mentally go up towards the thighs and relax your leg muscles.
- Relax the pelvis and unwind any tension that you might feel around the hips.
- Relax your lower back muscles, middle back muscles and finally, upper back and neck muscles.
- Focus on your neck and go back up to the skull.
- Relax your facial muscles, your cheeks, jaws and even the tongue.

Enjoy this relaxing state for a few minutes by focusing on physical sensations.

Practice #20 - Relax before bedtime

Tonight, relax and calm your body and mind before going to sleep.

An efficient method to calm the mind and prepare it for a good night's sleep consists of practising a relaxation technique such as deep breathing, a body scan or visualising a peaceful setting (explained above).

How will you sleep tonight?

CHAPTER II

STIMULATE YOUR VITALITY

Practice #21 - Stretch

Start your day by stretching for 5 minutes.

When you stretch your main muscle groups (back, arms, neck and legs), you are in touch with your physical dimension and energize your body. The flexibility of your muscles also contributes to joint mobility (ankles, knees, hips, shoulders, elbows, wrists). It´s like greasing wheels! For long-lasting mobility, try to practice these stretching exercises from this day forward. Your future self you will thank you!

How will you feel when you start your day with 5 minutes stretching exercises?

Follow the guide

- Standing up with both feet hips-width apart, stretch both arms upwards, interlink your fingers and press your palms upwards.
- Tuck in your chin and feel your neck stretch.
- Let go the left arm and stretch your right side by tilting the top of your body to the left - your right hip pushes to the right. Do the same for the other side.
- Stand up and grab a knee with both hands. Staying upright, pull the knee up to your chest. Knees together, keeping your balance on the standing leg, catch the foot by the back and bring the heel to your buttock. Do the same for the other side.
- Lastly, legs hips-width apart and feet slightly open, bend your knees and place your hands on your knees. Switch movements to articulate your spine: inhale as you arch your back and exhale as you curve your spine.
- Standing up, roll your shoulders back 3 times.

Great job! You are ready to start the day!

What if this were you?

Stéphanie is 27 years old. After graduating as a biologist, she decided to pursue her studies and started a doctorate under the guidance of a professor she esteems. She has been married for two years and is the mother of eleven-month old Nicolas. The ambitious and motivated mum is passionate about her doctorate and devotes a lot of energy to it. Since her son was born, Stéphanie feels that she is constantly in a life transition and can´t seem to find a healthy routine. She runs from day-care to laboratory, works hard during the day to spend every minute she can with her son once home. Evenings are short... and nights too, since Nicolas often wakes at night. Stéphanie has not practiced any sport since she was pregnant and doesn't take any time for herself, devoting her rare free time to her husband and son.

Without being completely worn out, Stéphanie is exhausted and doesn't feel content. Life does not match her hopes. She decides to change things and to start exercising again, after having stopped for more than two years. To ensure that exercising becomes a habit, she gets up ten minutes earlier each morning and stretches - no more, no less. After a few days, Stéphanie can feel the benefits of her 10-minute' resilient practice. Without it being a miracle cure, she appreciates these moments during which she can reconnect with her inner-self that have become part of her daily routine.

Stretching exercises are a simple and effective way of reconnecting to the physical dimension. By giving everything to her family and doctorate, Stéphanie had a tendency to forget herself. With some stretching exercises, she is now mindful of her body, stimulates her blood flow and increases her energy level.

Practice #22 - Enjoy a nutritious breakfast

Today, take some time to prepare a smart and healthy breakfast.

Include some protein (yoghurt, eggs or wholegrain cereals) in your breakfast to enjoy the right level of energy to start the day, to stay alert and attentive.

Research published by the University of Missouri[1] demonstrated that a protein-rich breakfast reinforces the feeling of fullness

1 H. Leidy, University of Missouri, "Consuming High-Protein Breakfasts Helps Women Maintain Glucose Control", 2014.

(satiety) and tends to reduce food consumption at lunchtime. Protein boosts the peptide YY production, a hormone that regulates appetite and sends a satiety signal to the brain.

Moreover, protein boosts alertness and cognitive capacity. Neurones need fat and carbohydrates but communicate together thanks to protein. Protein constitutes enzymes, neurotransmitters and hormones that convey messages allowing brain dictated tasks to be accomplished. Eating protein at breakfast triggers brain alertness. Therefore, in the evening when you want to calm your brain to favour a restorative and serene sleep, an excess of proteins is not recommended.

What will you have for breakfast today?

Practice #23 - Schedule walking meetings

Today, replace a traditional sitting-down meeting with a walking meeting.

Changing context stimulates creativity and inspires new ideas. It creates a break in your workday and contributes to staying in shape! Talking and walking side by side puts people at ease, leading to a positive working spirit.

What meeting will you walk today?

What if this were you?

Having recently started working for a growing SME, Géraldine works on several transversal projects. Like many, Géraldine spends a large part of her days sitting down in meetings. Although she uses public transportation to get to the office, she spends most of her day sitting.

Recognizing the benefits of exercise on physical health, mood and concentration, Géraldine invites her team to do walking meetings when there are two to four participants. She soon realises that these walking meetings are efficient and constructive. Her co-workers quickly latch on to this practice that has since spread to other departments.

On average, office workers spend 9 hours per day sitting down, i.e., more than the recommended 6 to 8 hours of restorative sleep. By doing walking meetings, Géraldine includes some exercise into her workday. She does not only feel physically better but is more productive too! Apple founder Steve Jobs (who died in 2011) and Facebook CEO Mark Zuckerberg are famous examples of leaders who integrated this practice in their everyday lives. A 2014 study by Stanford University[2] shows that creativity increases by an average 60%

2 M. Oppezzo, D. Schwartz, "The positive effect of walking on creative thinking", American Psychology Association, 2014.

when people are moving rather than sitting down. Great philosophers of Antiquity including Socrates and Aristotle were often seen deliberating the world as they strolled between the colonnades of the Lyceum, the school of philosophy founded by Aristotle.

Practice #24 - Walk up the stairs

Avoid the lift today: walk up the stairs instead.

Climbing up stairs during the day significantly contributes to the recommended 30 minutes of daily exercise. You will feel invigorated and in better shape.

While you are certainly aware of the benefits of exercise on your physical health, do you realise just how much exercise also impacts your brain?

Munich's Max Planck institute outlined the 5 key impacts of exercise on the organ of thought.

1) **Anti-stress shield:** muscle cells that are solicited produce a protein that extracts stress factors from the blood. This could help prevent depression.

2) **Muscles boost the brain:** some proteins migrate from the solicited muscles towards the brain, where they act like a balm. The brain cells are fortified and the mental works quicker.

3) **Good for the grey matter:** regular physical exercise not only develops muscles but also certain parts of the brain and the quantity of neurotransmitters such as serotonin increases.

4) **Good for the memory:** physical activity leads to the development of new brain cells in the hippocampus. New neurons can store new memories.

5) **Re-boost the brain:** physical movement decreases electrical activity in a section of the prefrontal cortex and allows a regenerative pause in the reflection process. After that, its ability to absorb is greater!

How many flights of stairs will you walk up today?

Practice #25 - Savour a healthy snack

Today, take some time to enjoy a healthy a snack: a piece of fresh fruit, a few nuts, raw vegetables or a square of dark chocolate.

Healthy snacking is good for the body, reduces hunger pangs, helps fight weight gain, regulates mood and stimulates the brain. A healthy snack not only provides sustainable energy, but also helps avoid the fatigue related to snacking on sugary foods.

What healthy snack will you take with you today?

Practice #26 - Host a stand-up meeting

Today, grab an opportunity to have a stand-up meeting.

Standing participants are more inclined to pay attention. Meetings are not only shorter, but often more efficient. Researchers[3] demonstrated that stand-up meetings not only reduce the

3 Knight, Baer, "Get Up, Stand Up: The Effects of a Non-Sedentary Workspace on Information Elaboration and Group Performance", Journal Social Psychological and Personality Science, 2014.

time spent in meetings but also encourage the active presence of participants, the exchange of ideas and collaborative spirit of a group. Finally, standing up brings dynamism to your body and is therefore healthier than sitting down.

During which meeting will you stand up today?

Practice #27 - Put some colour on your plate

Today, give special attention to preparing or choosing a colourful plate filled with assorted fruits and vegetables.

Different nutrients give foods different colours. Brain-sharpening anthocyanin give blueberries their bluish colour while immune system booster beta-carotene gives carrots their distinctive orange hue.

Using colours is the simplest way to detect antioxidants, chemical substances that are capable of preventing the toxic chain reactions provoked by free radicals. Like rust on metal, free radicals attack our bodies' cells and tissues and quicken ageing.

It should be noted that antioxidants provide an effective 3-hours of protection. In other words, the fruit you eat in the morning will no longer fight oxidation in the afternoon. This is why you should eat antioxidant-rich food regularly.

What colour is your lunch plate today?

Follow the guide

Here are a few simple tricks to help increase your consumption of antioxidants and put you on a healthy eating track:

- In restaurants, choose your dish with the "colours" criteria in mind. The more colour on your plate, the healthier your meal!
- Think about starting each meal with a mixed or green salad or with a vegetable soup to reinforce your oxidation-fighting capacities.
- Take a piece of fruit of some sliced raw vegetables to work.

Here are some very antioxidant-rich foods:

- Aubergine - beets - broccoli - carrots - lemon - spinach - kiwi fruit - egg yolk - apple - blueberries.

Remember: to function properly, your body needs the right balance of carbohydrates, proteins, good fats, lots of water and as many vitamins, minerals and antioxidants as possible.

Practice #28 - Take a powernap

Today, take a few minutes for a powernap.

A short nap (15-20 minutes) can alleviate your sleep debt. A powernap has considerable benefits: it improves concentration and performance without creating a feeling of lethargy when waking up and does not interfere with nocturnal sleep. Do you need to recharge your batteries? A powernap will boost your memory, cognitive functions, creativity and energy level.

In 1995, NASA[4] measured that a 26-minutes powernap improves performance by 34% and the alertness of pilots by

4 NASA, "Alertness management: strategic naps in operational settings", 1995.

54%. While powernaps are commonly practised in many Asian countries, it is still relatively new to the Western culture. Let's bet that this practice will become more common in the coming years! After Paris (*Zen Bar à Sieste*), a nap bar (*Pauzzz*) opened in Brussels' city centre in 2014. Companies and organisations increasingly incorporate a "relaxation area" to their work spaces, where staff is invited (and allowed) to rest.

Have you planned today's powernap?

What if this were you?

50-Year old Jeff successfully balances an interesting career with a fulfilling private life. Although many people admire and envy his energy, Jeff does not sleep enough. He comes home late at night and travels often, forcing him to wake up too early. For the past few years, Jeff has taken the habit to isolate himself from his colleagues to rest for 15 minutes. Concretely, he shuts his office door, pulls back his office chair, crosses his arms and places his forehead on his writs. Comfortably settled, he rests for a quarter of an hour. Jeff is power napping and - without understanding its mechanisms - feels the extent to which this resilient habit helps him sustain a high energy level in the afternoon, enabling him to assume his responsibilities without feeling tired.

With a powernap, Jeff not only rejuvenates his physical body but also calms his mind. Just to name a few famous "nappers": Napoleon used to nap on his horse; Winston Churchill could not miss his daily siesta and Salvador Dali practiced short naps to stimulate his creativity thanks to the hallucinations that sometimes emerge when falling asleep!
Many athletes take a rest in the middle of the day and planned daytime dozing is widespread among sailors to recover and remain vigilant because they cannot afford to sleep long hours.

Practice #29 - Adjust your posture

Today, take as many opportunities as you can to check and adjust your posture.

Good posture - seated or standing - makes breathing easier and increases concentration and cognitive capacities. Good posture also improves body image. People with good posture look better and naturally radiate more presence. Good posture also helps to avoid backache and increases self-confidence.

Imagine that a thread holds up your body and savour the benefits of good posture. When you are sitting down, try to push down the ischium humps (hip bones, under the buttocks) on the chair and to stretch your back, shoulders relaxed and head held high.

How is your posture now?

Practice #30 - Walk more

Today, walk more up to the recommended 10000 steps a day (using a pedometer or an App).

Walking is not only good for the health but also for the mind: being active boosts the production of endorphins - also known as well-being hormones - in the blood, reducing stress and anxiety. Our sedentary lifestyle provokes easily avoidable aches and pains. Like for any other key performance indicators, measuring supports progress.

But why 10000 steps? This value comes from a Japanese pedometer sold in Japan during the Tokyo 1964 Olympic games when a Japanese company created a "man-po-kei", a pedometer ("Man" means "ten thousand", "Po" means "step" and "Kei" designates the word "Meter" or "Gauge"). Presented as the reference value for physical activity, 10000 steps a day matches active lifestyles and is used by many public health authorities.

Let's emphasize that this measure is an average calculated for a medium-size, medium-bulk adult practicing average physical activity. You should not be obsessed to reach a goal in terms of number of steps, which should ideally be adapted for each person.

When will you go for a walk today?

Practice #31 - Feed your brain

Boost your mental faculty today!

Research demonstrates that specific healthy foods for the brain can strengthen memory, create more clarity and contribute to overall health. Although there are no miracle ingredients to instantly boost brain capacity, regularly enriching your diet with specific foods can help you function optimally.

What brain food will you eat today?

Follow the guide

- Dried fruit (raisins, dried apricots) and nuts (almonds, hazelnuts, walnuts) are particularly rich in minerals and micronutrients such as zinc which, if deficient can hinder learning capacity, memorisation and attention.
- Fatty fish (sardines, mackerels, herring, salmon) are the main providers of omega-3 fatty acids, which play a key role in memory and neurons.

- Organ meats (liver, kidneys, sweetbreads) deserve respect! These unpopular foods are rich in iron, which transports oxygen to the brain helping memorisation and concentration.

Practice #32 - Stand on one leg and keep your balance

Today, take some time and balance your body on one leg for 30 seconds before changing sides.

Staying balanced forces your muscles to stabilise and puts your abdominal muscles to work. Keep your balance while brushing your teeth or shaving in the morning.

Balancing on one leg can also help you feel more grounded and self-confident. Not only is it good for the body, but for your neurons too since it strengthens communication between muscles and the brain. This can prove very helpful as you grow older... i.e., now!

How stable are you on one leg?

Practice #33 - Hold the plank pose

Take a minute today to hold the plank pose.

It only takes between 15 seconds and a few minutes to do the plank pose. This exercise uses all the abdominal muscles: the right abdominal muscles (which - with work and perseverance - can create the "six-pack" effect), the oblique muscles (which will help fight "love handles") and the transverse abdominal muscles (the deepest and most important of all abdominal muscles, which are essential for good back health and posture).

How long can you hold the plank pose today?

Follow the guide

- To hold the plank pose, lean on your forearms to form a straight plank. More experienced yogees can try to hold the plank pose on their hands, without compromising the straightness of the posture.
- Keep your abdominal muscles tight.
- Look at the floor and keep your neck aligned with your spine.
- Push your heels backwards and the tip of your head forward, visualising a straight line linking these extremities.
- Breathe slowly and hold the posture for a few seconds or a few minutes, depending on your ability and need for a challenge at that precise moment!

It´s one of the best exercises for the abdominal belt and for overall muscle strengthening, which are key to good posture and increased presence. Every exercise can restore your good mood, the plank like all others!

Practice #34 - Sharpen your senses

Today, use all of your senses during your contact with others, at home and at work.

Your five senses - sight, sound, smell, taste and touch - are extraordinarily complex. They all work together to provide you information about your surroundings and allow you to appreciate relationships more intensely. The effectiveness of your senses is affected by factors such as age and illness.

Using all of your senses is an efficient practice to live in the present moment. Moreover, looking and listening attentively develops empathy, which strengthens social skills and improves relationships. It´s a win-win practice both at home and at work!

Will you keep your eyes and ears wide open today?

Practice #35 - Take a real lunch break

Today, spend at least half an hour for lunch, away from your desk.

Are you sometimes tempted to continue working to go home early without taking a lunch break? Do you wolf down a sandwich in your car between two meetings or while reading your emails on your computer? While you believe that you are saving time by zapping your lunch break, you may often lose it in terms of efficiency, resulting in fatigue and loss of concentration.

Look at the evidence: to stay on top, you need to take a few breaks every day, and that includes a lunch break. You are forcing your body to move and you clear your mind. Lunch breaks are the ideal opportunity to reconnect with colleagues. Take your lunch break away from your desk, not only do you deserve it, but you will likely be more efficient in the afternoon!

When will you take your lunch break today?

Practice #36 - Take a bite of (really) dark chocolate

Today, avoid mid-afternoon fatigue with a bite of really (very) dark chocolate (70% + cocoa).

It is not often that something that tastes delicious is good for you. Chocolate is an exception to this rule! Dark chocolate provides potassium, copper, magnesium and iron, which help reduce the risk of cardiovascular disease, anaemia, hypertension and heart conditions. Cocoa also contains theobromine and caffeine, substances that increase short-time concentration. Lastly, dark chocolate contains several chemical components - including phenylethylamine - that helps the brain release endorphins, making you happier!

How about treating your brain to a bit of (really dark) chocolate today?

Practice #37 - Eat (a bit more) slowly

Today, pay close attention to your eating habits and force yourself to eat slowly.

By eating slowly, you are giving your body the opportunity to receive the signal of fullness sent by the brain, which takes about 20 minutes. Research[5] indicates that eating slowly

5 Journal of the Academy of Nutrition and Dietetics, 2014.

increases the feeling of satiety and limits cravings in the hours following the meal.

Moreover, eating slowly is an invitation to eat more mindfully: focus your attention on the present, become aware of sensations, tastes, textures and smells. Mindful eating invites you to savour each bite and to transform mealtimes into moments of peace in your busy day.

Will you eat your next meal mindfully?

Practice #38 - Hold a "Power Pose"

Today, hold a "power pose" before a difficult conversation or an important meeting.

Amy Cuddy, associate professor at Harvard Business School, demonstrated the benefits of a good posture on your physiology and body chemistry, which in turn affects your mind, feelings and confidence. Holding a power pose can increase testosterone- the "domination hormone" - and decrease cortisol - the "stress hormone" - in the brain.

For her research, Amy Cuddy[6] studied the body language of power and domination in the animal world and in interactions between humans. The sensation of power manifests itself on the outside through the expansion of the body, as though it wanted to occupy more space. Animals stretch and grow. Peacocks make a wheel to demonstrate their power. Conversely, humans and other animals tend to look smaller and clam up when they are in a fragile position, shrinking into themselves as though it would reduce the threat.

6 A. Cuddy, "The benefits of power posing before a high-stakes social evaluation", Harvard Business School, 2012.

The psychologist asked one group to practise some expansion poses for two minutes. She instructed another group to take a vulnerability pose: huddled up, shrunk over a table, arms crossed, one arm on the neck, etc. Saliva tests demonstrated a 20% rise in the testosterone level of those who adopted a power pose; For the same participants, the level of cortisol dropped by approximately 25% rising 15% for those in a powerlessness pose. Here is proof of the almost-immediate hormonal change induced by our posture. These hormonal changes influence our brain, generating confident assurance or powerlessness.

Get in the habit of holding a power pose before an important meeting. In a meeting room, your kitchen, your office or even in the toilets! By increasing self-confidence and managing pressure more serenely, you are programming your brain for success.

What is your favourite power pose?

Follow the guide

The ideal power pose allows stretching out and occupying more space. Here are 3 examples to try before your next important meeting:

- **Standing up, feet hips-width apart, open your arms towards the sky in a V.**
- **Sitting down, interlink your fingers and place your hands behind your head, opening up your elbows to the outside.**
- **Standing up, feet spread wider than the hips, put your hands on the hips and open your chest.**

Practice #39 - Wake up at the same time every day

This weekend, wake up at the same time as you do during the week. When you wake up at different times during the week than on weekends, you impose a sort of jet lag on your body, a "social" jet lag. To function correctly, the body maintains a stable internal environment. This is called homeostasis. When it detects a time-zone change - whether real or artificial, it responds and adjusts.

By switching back to weekday hours again on Monday morning, you send a new signal to your body - trained like a soldier - that will adapt to help you "function" as best as possible. This natural adaptation system uses considerable energy and has physiological consequences.

Consider your waking hour as a metabolic starter. By stabilising wake-up time, you initiate the ideal physiological conditions to cultivate your energy throughout the week and avoid the Monday energy drop.

At what time will you set your alarm clock this weekend?

What if this were you?

Patrice is a young barrister hoping to become an associate this year. The heavy workload continues to increase after three lawyers left without being replaced. Days start early and end late... Patrice impatiently waits for Friday night to come. Patrice releases a lot of pressure when he goes out at the weekend, and loves his Saturday and Sunday morning' lie-ins. While his alarm clock rings at 6:30 every weekday morning, Patrice sleeps in until at least 11:00 at the weekend.

He believes that he is recovering the sleep debt accumulated during the week. He loves his lie-ins but is not as fond of returning to the weekly routine! Patrice feels exhausted on Monday mornings, which makes the start of the week more difficult than it has to be.

Understanding the biology of better sleep, Patrice decides to regularise his waking time and to experiment this practice for one month. He wakes up every day at 6:30, during weekends. Without giving up his Friday night outings, he integrated a power-nap into his Saturday and is careful to recover his sleep debt by going to bed earlier that night. After 3 weeks, Patrice is amazed by the impact of this new habit. He feels in better physical shape and enjoys the longer weekends... as he has now more time to do things on Saturday and Sunday mornings. The experience is a success and Patrice has incorporated this new habit in his daily routine

Although he was sceptical at first, Patrice quickly sensed the benefits of a regular waking time. More aware of the implications of his lie-ins on his physiology, he decided to spare his body and to manage his own vitality better.
His energy level is stable and he does not feel the early week fatigue syndrome.

Practice #40 - Prepare for sleep

Tonight, schedule a sleep preparation phase and spend some quiet time before going to bed.

Sleep is a basic body need. It represents an indispensable recuperation time to function optimally, physically and psychologically. According to a health survey conducted in Switzerland[7], a quarter of the population suffers from sleeping

7 Office fédéral de la statistique, "Troubles du sommeil dans la population", Enquête suisse sur la santé, 2012.

troubles and 8 out of 100 people take sleeping pills. Several factors can impair sleep or cause an agitated night, including excessive stimulation before bed.

Sleep is organised in 4 to 6 cycles of 90 minutes or so (called ultradian rhythms). We shift from one cycle to the next progressively before entering a phase of deep sleep. By calming down your physiology and preparing your brain for this rest period, you increase the odds of a rejuvenating night. Our ancestors intuitively understood this "cool-down" phase and spent their evenings around a fire. As it slowly extinguished, it created the ideal environment to fall asleep peacefully. Today, as we are constantly stimulated and exposed to artificial light, we need to put a sleep preparatory phase in place, more than ever before.

Creating a ritual (for instance: a relaxing bath, a cup of herbal tea, some breathing exercise or meditation), staying away from screens, limiting intellectual stimuli that agitate the brain are winning strategies with which to experiment!

聽

CHAPTER III

ENGAGE YOUR EMOTIONS

Practice #41 - Listen actively

Today, be mindful of the benefits of active listening.

Concentrate on the person who is speaking without interrupting. Beyond words, look at their body language, facial expression(s) and tone of voice. Active listening develops empathy and creates trust. It is a mark of respect, which helps focus on the conversation.

The Chinese ideogram for "listening" is very instructive: it consists of several components referring to the ears, eyes, attention and heart. A lovely and wise symbol!

Who will you actively listen today?

Follow the guide

To practise active listening, follow these steps and transform your listening skills:

- **Be wholly in the present moment.**
- **Focus your attention on the person you are with.**

- Active listening starts by keeping quiet! Look beyond words by observation: pay attention to non-verbal signals such as silence, tone of voice, posture and expressions.
- Show your interest by nodding, looking into the person's eyes or subtle verbal encouragements.
- You can then ask "open questions" to encourage self expression . You can also ask "closed questions" to help clarify thoughts.
- Use other words to rephrase the essence of what has been said, ensuring sound understanding and showing the person that s/he was listened to, heard and understood.

By demonstrating active listening, you are creating a space of trust to cultivate healthy and constructive relationships.

Practice #42 - Give positive feedback

Today, take one minute to give positive feedback to a friend or colleague.

Most people do not take the time to provide positive feedback during a busy day. Yet, when it is given appropriately, positive feedback has countless benefits and creates positive emotions for giver and receiver alike.

Positive feedback also allows to strengthen an appropriate behaviour. When feedback is genuine, direct and based on behaviours rather than on the person (I would like to congratulate you for what you did/achieved), it is a powerful motivator!

Who will you encourage today?

Practice #43 - Be grateful or practice WWW

Tonight, think about what you feel grateful for. Take a moment to practice the WWW exercise and ask yourself: *What Went Well* today?

The evening is the ideal moment to reflect and cultivate gratitude. By doing this exercise daily, you shift your thinking towards the positive aspects of your life, including the people to whom you are grateful...

Gratitude is one of the pillars of positive psychology. It´s not about ignoring what is challenging but about willingly focusing your attention on the positive events of each day. Psychologist Robert Emmons[1], a researcher in psychology at the University of California, noted that people capable of listing to the reasons why they felt good were more active and stress-resistant.

What went well for you today?

What if this were you?

Life is hard... thinks 46-year old Bruno, who has been out of work for 11 months. Bruno co-parents his two daughters (10 and 12) with his ex-wife. Every time the girls go back to their mother´s, he can´t seem to recapture his faith in the future or joy of living. His days are paced with work interviews, broken hopes and disappointments. Bruno is not happy with a life that does not match his dreams. During a work-training module, an external consultant tells him about the benefits of gratitude and encourages him to practice a gratitude exercise each day for the following two weeks. Bruno decides to play along and

1 Robert Emmons, "Why Gratitude is good", University of California, 2011.

finds something to be grateful each night: a coffee with a friend, an interview that went well, an interesting conversation, smiles on his daughters' face... After a few days, Bruno feels more positive and happier. Astonished by the impact of this simple exercise, he decides to practice gratefulness daily.

◗ Bruno quickly felt the benefits of gratitude, which stimulates positive emotions. By focusing his attention on the positive events of the day, Bruno soothes his mind, preventing his daily worries from keeping him up at night.

Practice #44 - Thank a colleague or a friend

Take a minute to say thank you to a friend or colleague today.

Perhaps you have a tendency to underestimate the impact of thanking someone at work. Use sincere words, whether orally or in writing. Be specific and show that you really mean every word you use.

When you express gratitude, the person you are thanking feels recognised, valued and is also more likely to help you in the future...

Who will you thank today?

Practice #45 - Celebrate a success

Today, take a moment to celebrate a - major or minor - success with your team.

When did you last gather your team to celebrate a success: a decisive step in a project, the accomplishment of a crucial objective or any other achievement by a team member? If you have to think for more than 30 seconds, this practice should help you remember just how important it is to celebrate every step that paves the path of success.

Although it is important to work hard to achieve objectives, it is also essential to recognise and celebrate the stages leading to a goal. Every contribution to achieve a team mission is a success worthy of celebration. It boosts morale and creates positive emotions, powerful support for anyone.

Which success will you celebrate today?

Practice #46 - Write down your emotions

Today, take a minute to jot down your emotions on a piece of paper.

Self-awareness is key for resilient individuals and it begins with the ability to identify one's own emotions. Our vocabulary is often lacking when we have to identify and name emotions. Until now, most educational systems have not nurtured this type of exercise. Yet, what cannot be named tends to be ignored. Today, science demonstrates that destructive emotions that are not managed well may lead to physical illnesses.

Making a habit of writing down the emotions felt (ideally every day) broadens the emotional vocabulary and builds self-awareness. This contributes to improved self-control, healthier relationships, a better health and a more fulfilling life.

What emotions did you feel today?

Follow the guide

- **Emotions are human physiological manifestations in the face of internal (personal) and external (linked to the environment) events. Since they are unavoidable, they should be acknowledged, understood, and managed.**
- **Enrich your emotional vocabulary by identifying each so-called "basic" emotion (identified by American psychologist Paul Ekman[2] who pioneered the study of emotions and their relation to facial expressions): anger, joy, fear, sadness, surprise, disgust and every nuanced secondary emotion that you may have felt today.**

---

2 Paul Ekman is an American psychologist who pioneered the study of emotions and their relation to facial expressions.

- Write down the words that seem to best translate your feelings.
- Take a moment to decide whether this emotion is functional (it helps me function) or dysfunctional/destructive (it does not help/serve me). Note: a negative emotion is not always dysfunctional. In case of grief, sadness - a negative emotion - is functional and a compulsory step in the healing process.

This exercise is not aimed to block dysfunctional or negative emotions, but rather to recognise and accept them, reinforcing self-awareness, a foundation of resilience.

Practice #47 - Smile

Today, take every opportunity to smile.

Smiling initiates a virtuous circle. Its effects are not limited to the brain but also include behaviour and body. Studies[3] suggest that a smile - even forced - has a positive effect on mood, decreases stress and strengthens the immune system. When you smile, you stimulate the production of serotonin, a hormone that plays a key role in emotional balance. Some call it the "anti-depression" agent.

Research by the University of Pittsburgh[4] (Pennsylvania, United States) indicates that women who smile most are perceived as more trustworthy than those whose facial expression is unsmiling. What happy news!

How about smiling right now?

---

3 TL. Kraft, "Grin and bear it: the influence of manipulated facial expression on the stress response", University of Kansas, 2012. Dunbar et al, "Social laughter is correlated with an elevated pain threshold", The Royal Society Publishing, 2011.

4 K. Schmidt, Levenstein R, Ambadar Z, "Intensity of smiling and attractiveness as facial signals of trustworthiness in women", University of Pittsburgh, 2012.

Follow the guide

If – like many others – you have heard about serotonin, dopamine or adrenalin without really understanding the nature or function of these molecules, take a moment to read these simple explanations:

Neurotransmitters are molecules conveying information between neurons. Produced in your brain, these chemical "couriers" impact attention, memory, mood and stress. These six neurotransmitters boast the most influence on neurons:

- **Serotonin** creates a fertile ground for cautious, reflected, calm behaviour and also regulates mood. The brain uses serotonin to make melatonin, the sleep-inducing hormone. To stimulate the production of serotonin, eat tryptophan-rich food like brown rice, legumes, avocados or porridge.
- **Dopamine** is often associated with pleasure and alertness. It affects muscle movements and plays a role in the optimal functioning of the kidneys and heart. Precursors of melatonin are phenylalanine and tyrosine, two amino acids (components of food proteins) found in protein-rich food such as cottage cheese and eggs.
- **Noradrenalin** creates favourable conditions for excitation, alertness, learning and sleep. It is a precursor of adrenalin, one of the neurotransmitters of the sympathetic nervous system.
- **GABA** (Gamma-Amino Butyric Acid) triggers relaxation. The most common neurotransmitter in the brain slows down the transmission of nervous signals, thus calming the brain and regulating anxiety. Low and moderate glycaemic index food distributing glutamine – an amino acid precursor of the GABA – should be consumed: almonds, bananas, broccoli, walnuts, and lentils.
- **Acetylcholine** favours memorisation and plays a role in controlling movements. It is the only neurotransmitter

in this list that is not made out of an amino acid, but of a substance found in food: choline. The best sources of choline include: egg yolk, soy, wheat germ or cruciform (such as kale, cabbage, broccoli or turnips).

- **Adrenalin** works as a neurotransmitter of the sympathetic nervous system. It activates the whole body to confront danger or when emotions are very intense. A chronically high adrenalin rate leads to anxiety, acute fatigue, dwindling attention and depression. To counter these detrimental effects, magnesium-rich foods should be consumed, including green vegetables, legumes, seafood, dried fruit, whole cereals and chocolate.

Practice #48 - Participate actively in discussions

Many individuals grumble about excessive meetings that stop them from working on their projects. Many attend meetings reluctantly or passively. Yet, lack of participation is an obvious obstruction to an effective meeting. Taking part actively is not always easy particularly when you are tired or have little interest in the agenda, but this is a critical condition for a successful meeting.

Interactions enrich and justify the reason of a meeting. By making comments, asking questions or putting forth suggestions, you are demonstrating your commitment and strengthening your assertiveness. Moreover, this behaviour supports (and justifies!) your presence.

What if this were you?

Naturally introverted, Isabelle is not very talkative - discreet even - both in her private and work life. Within the framework of her job, Isabelle works hand in hand with different divisions and attends many transversal meetings. Passionate about her job, she does not much enjoy these endless conversations and finds that these meetings tend to be inefficient. As she recently joined the organisation, she does not like to intervene and often ends up staying quiet during entire discussions.

Conscious that boredom is by no means an ideal companion, Isabelle mindfully decides to take part in working discussions with her colleagues. Her questions prove refreshing and relevant. The team enjoys her interventions and involve her more. Isabelle quickly feels that her active participation creates a virtuous circle. She decides to express herself more often during family reunions and during evenings with her friends. By talking more, she is also more present for those around her.

By participating more actively, Isabelle reveals her qualities and strengthens her self-confidence. She creates more contacts with her colleagues, which makes collaboration easier and increases the pleasure of working together. At home, active participation in discussions is a successful way to make yourself available and attentive to your family.

Practice #49 - Use humour

Today, grab an occasion to use humour .

Humour is a powerful weapon that dissipates tensions and creates bonds between people. Used appropriately, humour helps de-dramatizing a situation and stimulates a positive mindset.

Researchers have demonstrated the benefits of humour on anxiety, productivity and an overall sense of happiness. Entertaining leaders are also perceived as more convincing and assertive.

French comedian Gérard Jugnot uses a witty metaphor to prove the benefits of laughter. *"Rain is like windscreen wiper, it won't stop the rain but helps you to move on"*.

How will you add a touch of humour to your interactions today?

Practice #50 - Say hello

Today, take a minute to say hello to your family and greet your colleagues when at work.

Saying hello is the root of all social interactions. It is one of the first expressions of politeness that parents teach their children when they start socialising. It creates a positive contact with others.

You are probably using this practice naturally at home, but do you take the opportunities to do so at the office? Saying hello - a very simple practice - often sorely lacks in the work environment and not without consequences. Greeting is the basis for acknowledging the existence of other. It only takes a few seconds to assert the type of relationship you are about to establish.

Do not underestimate the power of a "hello" on your colleagues. When you greet someone , they feel recognised. Some teams shared just how much the application of this technique between co-workers profoundly improved the work atmosphere. To greet someone genuinely, look at the person in the eyes, smile and say hello. It will not cost you a thing and can cheer up that person - and you - to start the day optimally.

Who will you greet this morning?

Practice #51 - Create a quick win

Today, find an opportunity for a quick win.

Big changes or major projects take time, sometimes months if not years. When your list of tasks is endless and the efforts complex, you risk running out of steam, which can lead to a drop in motivation.

Quick wins energise and give impetuous to an effort. Finalising a report, making that phone call you are constantly putting off, tidying up your desk, finishing a presentation, answering an email or any other - measurable and easy to reach goal - is a quick win. It will give the necessary incentive to your morale and help you regain some motivation.

Which quick win will you create today?

Practice #52 - Admire nature

Today, stop for a moment and admire the beauty of nature.

Connecting with nature is soothing, stimulates positive emotions and feeds a feeling of gratitude. When observing, you are paying attention and are fully in the present moment.

Researcher Jia Wei Zhang[5], of Berkeley University (California) conducted a study involving more than 1000 adults aimed at measuring the correlation between a connection with nature and a feeling of well-being. He found that people connected with nature tend to be more satisfied with their life in general and have higher self-esteem, if and only if they are emotion-

---

5 JW. Zhang, "Engagement with natural beauty moderates the positive relation between connectedness with nature and psychological well-being", The Journal of Environmental Psychology, 2014.

ally engaged with nature. He thus proposes a subtle distinction between a connection with nature and an emotional perception of its beauty.

In other words, it is not enough to immerse yourself in nature; you have to be able to perceive the beauty it reveals. The capacity for wonderment is a competence to cultivate.

How will nature amaze you today?

Practice #53 - Appreciate a touch of lightness

Today, take the initiative of adding a touch of lightness to your day.

Whilst approaching your work seriously, don't forget that excess solemnity can prove counter-productive. When it becomes cumbersome, it dampers your creativity and reduces the field of possibilities. Letting go and breathing some lightness into your day can prove constructive for you and those around you.

Swiss philosopher Alexandre Jollien invites people to stop taking themselves too seriously. *"The tragedy consists in being thrown into a world we did not choose. Fear is the temptation to be rigid. Wisdom consists in finding lightness where chaos usually reigns"*. This is an invitation to use some humour, to read something funny or do something out of the ordinary.

How will you instil in some lightness into your life today?

Practice #54 - Read facial expressions

Today, pay particular attention to the emotions of others, grasping every opportunity to decipher their facial expressions.

According to studies by American psychologist Paul Ekman, facial expressions give clear indications of the emotions at play. Micro-expressions activate and regulate emotions. Paul Ekman demonstrated that such micro-expressions are recognisable in every culture, regardless of history or social context. People in France have the same expression of sadness as indigenous populations in Papua New-Guinea who never watched television or opened a magazine. Similarly, Paul Ekman demonstrated that people who were blind from birth have the same facial expres-

sions as the non-blind, without having ever seen the face of another person.

You can thus perceive information on the feelings of the person facing you and knowingly pick the best possible response. By reading facial expressions, you open your social engagement system and cultivate empathy, a crucial factor for constructive relationships.

Are you ready to open the door to empathy?

Follow the guide

A micro-expression is a brief - less than a second - facial expression depending on the emotions a person is experiencing. American psychologist Paul Ekman identified seven universal micro-expressions: joy, sadness, fear, disgust, anger, surprise and contempt.

Here are some tips to identify the emotions revealed by micro-expressions of the person in front of you:

- Joy: lips are pulled up towards the ears, cheeks are up, upper teeth are apparent, upper lids are lowered, and eyes are wrinkled, producing small lines around the eyes.
- Sadness: the corners of the mouth drop, the inside of eyebrows goes up, lower lids drop and the eyes stare into space.
- Fear: the mouth is agape, the upper lids rise and lower lids stretch at the corner of the eye, eyebrows rise and come close together.
- Disgust: the upper lip rises; the nose wrinkles and nostrils go up, eyebrows frown and the chin contracts.
- Anger: Lips are tight, eyebrows frown and go downwards, the lion's wrinkle (between the brows) appears and nostrils dilate.
- Surprise: The mouth opens slightly, eyes go wide and eyebrows move up.
- Contempt: a smirk appears on one side of the mouth - often the left, as the right side of the brain controls emotions. Sometimes, the chin lifts up and the head slightly tilts backwards. Note: the micro-expression translating contempt is the only asymmetrical micro-expression.

Following the indications above, practice in front of a mirror and become familiar with these micro-expressions that make wonderful emotional cues.

Practice #55 - Have lunch and create a connection

Today, invite a colleague for lunch and take time to connect.

For many of us, the lunch break goes out the window as the increased working pace has progressively reduced our midday break. However, lunch is the ideal moment to take a break in the middle of your day allowing you to rejuvenate. By inviting a colleague for lunch, you create a social connection, a major source of energy.

Who will you take to lunch today?

What if this were you?

Nicolas is a freelance journalist specialised in economic affairs. He works for a monthly magazine and loves the flexibility of his job. Once a week, Nicolas attends the editorial meeting but apart from this social weekly moment, he often works from home, which allows him to be available for his family. Nicolas loves his work but often feels lonely. Opportunities to share are rare and days are long. As he enjoys attending the editorial meetings, Nicolas recognises the importance of interacting with his friends and colleagues and realises that misses such moments. From then on, he decides to plan lunch meetings three times a week, giving him the opportunity to share and enjoy external stimulation. Such lunch breaks rekindle his energy and boost his motivation.

◗ By planning lunches with friends or colleagues, Nicolas cultivates social interactions. This increases the production of serotonin and contributes to emotional balance. Nicolas quickly reaps the benefits of this new practice. He enjoys himself, pleases his guests and increases his good mood - which benefits everyone around him.

Practice #56 - Spoil yourself

Today, create an occasion to spoil yourself and enjoy a moment of pleasure.

Some people are very good at grasping instants of happiness in their everyday lives despite the constraints and worries they encounter. Others feel guilty at the mere idea of pleasing/treating themselves. Who do you feel closest to?

Psychiatrist François Lelord stresses that feeling pleasure improves mood, decrease pressure and helps you to face adversity. *"Every time we feel pleasure, a reward system triggers the release of dopamine in the brain. This substance will lead to pleasant sensations, which motivates to renew the experience."*

Although little pleasures put some flavour in our lives, do they contribute to our happiness? It would seem so. Researcher Ed Diener[6] studied that the intensity of happiness sensations does not matter as much as the frequency of these sensations. Creating and appreciating simple pleasures seems to be a winning strategy. It is certainly more accessible and effective than waiting for Nirvana!

How will you spoil yourself today?

What if this were you?

An architect and the mother of three boys aged 8 to 16, Nathalie is an expert in the art of juggling her role as a mother, spouse and professional. In addition to this triad of roles, she is a good friend with a busy social life, a great sister in a family of four children and a helpful daughter to her

6 E. Diener, "Happiness is the frequency, not the intensity, of positive versus negative affects", Assessing Wellbeing - University of Illinois, 2009.

parents, whose health is slowly declining. 24-Hour days give Nathalie very little time to look after herself. She takes on her many roles but feels frustrated, as though something was missing. A friend warns her and encourages her to put some time aside for pleasurable moments, just for her. She reminds Nathalie of the safety instructions given on a plane, which advise passengers to put on their own oxygen mask before helping others in case of decompression in the aircraft cabin.

Nathalie decides to plan two 60-minutes "MT" (Me Time) slots every week. It's only a start but it changes everything. Twice a week, Nathalie treats herself: going to an exhibition, having dinner with a girlfriend, going for a walk or swimming - her favourite sport. This MT has become invaluable and gives her that extra boost of energy to fulfil her many roles with joy.

Nathalie has come to realise that she was better equipped to fulfil her tasks and responsibilities by frequently spoiling herself. Creating time for oneself regularly and sensibly is a healthy and essential resilient habit. Any feeling of guilt is quickly replaced with a feeling of well-being. You are glowing and your friends and family can enjoy the benefits of a happier you.

Practice #57 - Make someone happy

Today, create an occasion to make a friend or a colleague happy.

Busy, rushed or simply tired, regardless of the reason, you may sometimes forget to make someone happy. You will help yourself by helping others. Many researchers assert that being generous impacts the mental and physical life of the giver.

A 2008 experiment conducted by researcher Elizabeth Dunn[7] of the Vancouver British Columbia University consisted of

7 E. Dunnetal, "Spending Money on Others Promotes Happiness", Science, 2008.

giving a sum of money (10 dollars) to people, who were then free to keep or share it. The study demonstrated that those who shared their money with others felt happier. Conversely, those asked to keep the money felt a sense of shame that stimulated the production of stress hormone cortisol. Since excess cortisol is harmful to the body, the study suggests a correlation between generosity and health.

Who will you make happy today?

Practice #58 - Recall a happy memory

Today, take a moment to recall a happy experience.

Contrary to popular belief, nostalgia does not feed negative feelings but instead, it intensifies good mood as it leans on happy memories (travels, parties, sport challenges, school success, etc.) rekindling positive emotions.

By recalling happy memories, you are stimulating a pleasurable feeling of well-being. Dr Clay Routledge[8] of North Dakota University studied "nostalgia" and suggests that happy past experiences help take up the challenges of today by giving more meaning to life.

Which happy memory will you recall today?

Practice #59 - Anticipate good times

Today, cultivate a positive frame of mind by anticipating a happy event or positive experience that you are going to experience.

---

8 C. Routledge, "The Past Makes the Present Meaningful: Nostalgia as an Existential Resource", Journal of Personality and Social Psychology, 2011.

Research demonstrates that anticipating joy is good for the brain, emotions and physical health. When you anticipate something that you are looking forward to, the brain stimulates the production of dopamine - the well-being hormone - which tends to activate the behaviours that will allow you to enjoy the anticipated experience.

And what if that moment of happiness does not come? And what if this experience does not take place? When doubt arises, anxiety is not far behind. Could anticipating a happy event prove damaging? Experts agree that there are more advantages than risks in anticipating positive moments, even if they eventually do not happen...

American psychologist Greg Kushnick notes that anticipating positive events helps managing uncertainty better by stimulating hope and a feeling of control. If we consider the uncertainties that characterise today's working environment in countless sectors, this is a particularly welcome practice!

Which enjoyable future event will you anticipate today?

Practice #60 - Respond, don't react

Overcome impulsive reactions by giving a calm and firm response to an irritating person or situation.

Controlling impulses is a crucial competence for constructive relationships. Research in neuroscience helped to identify the impulse mechanism related to human survival. A lot quicker than a thoughtful response initiated by the pre-frontal cortex - the brain's decision centre - impulsive reactions are stimulated by the amygdala, two small glands at the core of your limbic brain. When feeling threatened, these glands activate a survival reaction: fight, flight or freeze.

The physiology immediately adapts. The level of adrenalin surges and activates the reply of your organism to a threatening stimulus. The heart beats quicker, blood pressure goes up, and muscles contract. If you bolt, blood circulation is activated in the legs and you run quicker than ever. If you are in a fight, the blood circulation in the upper body and the jaw is activated, thus accelerating oxygen distribution and magnifying your strength. When it is stimulated, the amygdala acts like a light switch that prevents access to the prefrontal cortex, stopping any reflection that could interrupt the process. You are no longer in charge: your amygdala is in control.

The same phenomenon can be witnessed when you "explode" with your colleagues or family, when words go beyond your thoughts, when you send an aggressive email that you regret five minutes later. A person or situation (a trigger) activates these many impulsive reactions, awakening your amygdala and driving you to a behaviour that you may regret. Along the way, you will have lost a considerable dose of energy and perhaps harmed your relationship with the person concerned.

Research demonstrates that a brief moment is enough to stop the activation of the amygdala and instead, stimulate the neuronal connection informing the prefrontal cortex of the presence of this "trigger". You will then choose the most appropriate response and will adopt a constructive behaviour. In other words, you refuse to be hijacked by your amygdala and respond calmly and firmly to the "trigger" (person/situation).

How do you feel when you can give a calm and firm response to the "trigger"?

Follow the guide

Being resilient does not mean being Zen at all times, nor accepting everything and never getting annoyed! It encourages you to use your awareness to choose the mindful response to the irritating factor ("trigger") whilst expressing your emotions calmly and firmly. Do not neglect this last step.

- Anticipate: know your triggers. In the next two weeks, write down the situations or persons that anger you. You will soon note that the same triggers repeat themselves.
- Breathe out: in the presence of a trigger, immediately stop the impulsive reaction and take time to exhale. This will give you the time needed to soothe your amygdala and stimulate your decision centre: the prefrontal cortex.
- Express: Choose a calm and firm response that you will express when in full control of yourself.

In the professional arena, impulsive individuals are toxic for their peers and can undermine the atmosphere of a team. Show a good example: give calm and firm responses to critical situations.

DIRECTION OF THE DAY

CHAPTER IV

TRAIN THE MIND

Practice #61 - Set an intention

Today, take a minute to set an intention that will steer your attitude throughout the day.

What were your first thoughts when you woke up? Do you realise their impact on the start of your day? This practical key will help clarify how you want to feel and act throughout the day. Set your intention!

Before starting any activity, decide what matters most today and the consistent behaviours in line with your values. Once the intention is clarified, you are better equipped to face the challenges of the day and to make better decisions using an «internal compass" to steer choices. Be open to what can help you honour an intention and be attentive as to what could prevent it.

How will you live this day?

Practice #62 - Work off-line

Today, plan to work off-line for a full hour. New technologies have become unavoidable and Internet cultivates an illusion of ubiquity, i.e., the capacity of being present in several different places at the same time. However, attention and presence are contingent to the capacity to concentrate.

Data on the use of Internet at work is alarming. A 2015 OLFEO[1] survey indicates that 44% of the time spent on Internet at work relates to personal matters, which impacts productivity, since a private use of internet at work represents a 10% drop in productivity!

A study published in the Harvard Business Review[2] in 2009 indicated that 85% of work emails are opened within 2 minutes. Many people are connected 24/7, constantly on the lookout for the next incoming message. In fact, when you send a message, do you not expect a quick reaction? This creates an expectation of instantaneity leaving little time and space for reflection.

Disconnecting from incoming messages helps you concentrate on the task at hand. Production increases while distractions decline. Working "off-line" ensures that you give your full attention to an immediate task or a colleague and supports your in the moment presence.

When will you work off-line today?

---

1 OLFEO, «La réalité de l'utilisation d'internet au bureau».

2 P. Hemp, "Death by information overload", Harvard Business Review, 2009.

What if this were you?

Laurence's job takes her far away from home three days a week, when she travels to other European countries and Asia. When she is not travelling, Laurence works from home, where she set up a workspace with an office connection. She spends most of her time working and is grateful to her stay-at-home husband who looks after their two children aged twelve and ten.

Although she would like to be more present and available for her teams and her family, Laurence is continuously connected. When she decides to work on a project, she is constantly interrupted by incoming messages or phone "alerts" reminding her to check her instant messaging system. When her children come home from school, she shifts from typing a text to getting after-school snacks, going from preparing dinner to reading a message. She finds it hard to concentrate during the day, except when she is on a plane for several hours at a time. Isolated from the world and in "flight mode", she can work effectively on her many projects. These off-line moments support her concentration. From then on, she decides to put in place an hour of off-line work per day. Laurence perceives this new habit as a crucial one in her routine.

◗ Taking advantage of these "compulsory" off-line moments during a flight, Laurence experiences the gain in time, concentration and energy inherent to off-line work. Since she restricts unfocused concentration from too many interruptions, that off-line hour becomes a key moment for daily reflection.

Practice #63 - Identify 3 key priorities

Take a minute to identify your 3 key priorities for the day.

When defining priorities, you shed light and steer your energy toward your most important things. Strategic business priorities are defined annually in many large companies before being translated into mid or short-term execution plans by different teams.

This system is not necessarily adapted to today's constantly evolving world, which is characterised by unpredictable changes challenging previously determined plans. Watch out, confusion is around the corner...

To maintain a clear light in a climate of uncertainty, it is crucial to identify daily priorities. The "top 3" of the day helps focus and conveys a satisfying sense of responsibility. You may not control the priorities chosen at the upper level of your organisation, but you can still decide every day, what to focus your attention on.

Which 3 key actions would you like to accomplish today?

Practice #64 - Transform adversity

Today, grab a chance to transform adversity into opportunity. What if it was a key resilience factor? In all its forms, adversity affects each one of us at various moments in life.

By making a clear distinction between what you can and cannot change, you are searching for an opportunity in the face of adversity. This positive mindset broadens the field of possibilities and stimulates creativity.

Obviously, some people are faced with major dramas or difficulties and it is essential to recognise - with compassion and humility - that this practice may at times prove insufficient.

Which opportunity will you create today?

Follow the guide

When adversity rears its head, ask yourself the following three questions and train your mind to approach it constructively:

- Will this still matter a year from now?

In Buddhist philosophy, nothing is permanent. Recognising that adversity - in its present and current form - is temporary very often lightens the burden, making it more bearable.

- What can I learn from this experience?

Good and bad life experiences are the best teachers you could hope for. The difficulties encountered are a huge source of learning that will help you grow.

- Which opportunity lies behind this difficulty?

Napoleon Hill[3] once said "Every adversity, every failure, carries with it the seed of an equal or greater benefit". If you look for the benefits of adversity, you are training the mind to create opportunities when facing difficulties.

Practice #65 - Unplug and be present

Today, take a moment to unplug from the virtual world and to be present, here and now.
Despite its inherent speed and flexibility, modern technology poses a significant risk of missing opportunities in the present moment. By unplugging from the virtual world, we bring our full attention to the present.

Are we still able to do that? Today's pervasive use of smart-

3 Napoleon Hill (1883-1970) is an American author specialised in self-help books.

phones urges more and more people to be connected to their device day and night. Are smartphones the drug of the century? A recent study[4] demonstrated that smartphone users check their phone on average 150 times a day. Moreover, they are incapable of staying away from their device for more than 6 minutes. In fact, most people start using their phone as soon as they wake up and check it last thing at night before going to sleep.

Such behaviour is not without consequence and proves harmful to both physical and mental health in the long term. Some people are even tense and anxious when they are away from their phone, a phobic anxiety called "nomophobia" (no mobile phobia). This simple practice invites you to reflect about your smartphone use habits and define a personal discipline to enjoy this extraordinary tool without becoming its slave.

For what or whom will you be present today?

What if this were you?

Hughes is a married father of two: a four-year-old daughter and two year old son. He works for the IT department of a company manufacturing office equipment. His wife Sophie is a doctor who works in a private practice from home and takes care of most family chores. Determined to adapt to the new demands of clients who increasingly purchase products on-line, Hughes' company is undergoing changes that increase the pressure on the IT department, which is at the front line of digital transformation. In this context, Hughes tends to work long hours and cannot truly disconnect when he gets home. He stays glued to his mobile phone and is easily annoyed by the noise of his children that prevent him from concentrating and answering yet another "urgent" message. During the family dinner, Hughes' daughter notices her dad typing

4 T. Ahonen, Mobile Telecoms Industry Review, Tomi Ahonen Almanac, 2017.

away on his phone and tells him "You're there but you're not there..." Hughes quickly realises that his attitude is pointless and decides that he will keep his phone away from the dinner table from now on. This moment of disconnection is now a moment of full-connection with the people he loves most.

By creating a physical distance between himself and his phone, Hughes has found a way to honour his wish of being truly present for his family. He focuses his full attention on his children, who immediately sense whether their father is there with just his body or with his body, head and heart.

Practice #66 - Tidy your workspace

Today, take some time to tidy up your desk.

How does your desk look like? There are two types of persons in terms of tidiness: tidy people who will sort out their files and office equipment each night and throw away dirty cups on the desk and the others, who are allergic to tidying up and who thrive in chaos! This key practice should remind everyone that a tidy desk suggests an organised mind. It helps keep your attention away from the many temptations and solicitations stemming from the overall mess and creates clarity. Tidying can also reduce sensations of stress, confusion or pressure.

Untidiness aficionados will be delighted to learn that a study[5] carried out by the University of Minnesota shows the link between an untidy desk and creativity.

You choose between order and disorder - whatever you need most right now!

Are you ready to tidy your desk? Or not?

5 K. Vohs et al., "Tidy desk or messy desk? Each has its benefits", Psychological Science, 2013.

Practice #67 - Watch your "info-diet"

Today, pay extra attention to your consumption and production of information.

Do you sometimes feel overwhelmed by excess information? Are you saturated by the mass of data? Today, information travels at the speed of light. It is accessible to all and is no longer exclusively for the educated. It may be astounding but, but like any progress, it also poses a risk: Information overload! Information overload (also known as "infobesity" or "infoxication" in Quebec) refers to the difficulty of understanding an issue and effectively making decisions when one is exposed to too much information.

The amount of information we absorb in a day is equivalent to what our ancestors processed in a lifetime. A 2010 study carried out by BASEX[6] (Management Science for the Knowledge Economy) concluded that 94% of respondents had already felt so overwhelmed by the mass of information that they experienced a feeling of incapacity.

When producing and consuming information consciously, we encourage presence and attention two key factors we know are key for success, don't we?

How will you feed the information thread today?

Follow the guide

Preventing infobesity means a more conscious consumption and production of information. These suggestions might help:

- **Save some "information-free" time between the moment you wake up and the time you start reading papers or surfing the web. Avoid stimulating or agitating your mind in the hour following waking up.**
- **Carefully choose media sources. Read articles from reliable sources and avoid the many distractions that will take over your attention, click after click.**
- **Identify a personal discipline for dealing with your emails (see practice #70) and – if you work in a team – define guidelines for the team: What is your email consultation policy during the day, in the evening, at weekends or during holidays? How quickly do we commit to respond to emails? Who do we CC in our messages?**

6 Basex, "Information overload calculation", Basex report, 2010.

- Reflect on your use of social media. Resist the temptation to plunge into social media (and to lose yourself) as soon as you have an idle minute. When you post something, pay attention to your intention.
- Respect a sleep preparation phase by staying away from screens. Do not stimulate your brain for 30 minutes before going to sleep. If your mind is calm, your night will be sweet!

Practice #68 - Dismiss thinking traps

Today, dismiss your thinking traps to foster a constructive mind.

We all know that some emotions prevent us from thinking clearly, compel us to elaborate anxiety-inducing thoughts or simply drive us mad. We all perceive events and situations through a different prism and we sometimes fall into thinking traps, which may lead to rumination and limit our potential. Regardless whether you are in a meeting or answering a tricky question, subject to an unpleasant remark from a family member, or in a traffic jam, your thoughts support a constructive mindset or conversely, a restrictive - even erroneous - reasoning.

Learning to dismiss your most frequent thinking traps limits the torments linked to dwelling and stimulates a constructive mindset. Likewise with empathy and care, observe other's thinking traps and see how you can help dismiss them.

How will you dismiss your most frequent thinking traps?

Follow the guide

Using this non-exhaustive list, become more aware of your thinking traps and use the suggested dismissal to train a constructive mindset.

Thinking traps	Dismissal
• Labelling, over generalising	Be specific, not personal
• Tunnel vision	Focus on big picture
• Personalising	Recognise the role of others
• Externalising, blaming	Be accountable
• Should / Must	Less rigid, more flexible thinking
• Jump to conclusions	Slow down: is there evidence?
• Mind reading	Check, clarify, question
• Emotional reasoning	Separate fact and feeling
• Catastrophizing / Awfulising	Put into context on a scale of 0 to 100
• Comparing	Link success to values / personal criteria

Practice #69 – Go on the balcony

Today, take a few minutes to take distance and be the observer of your own life.

Going to the balcony is an invitation to stop what you are doing, close your eyes and observe yourself at a given moment. In an environment where we tend to be over-stimulated, the capacity to take some distance whilst being in the moment is key to creating calm and clarity. There is nothing new in this ancestral practice other than the recent and numerous research proving the benefits of this practice and the increased need to cultivate calm in a demanding environment.

An increasing number of studies in neuroscience measure the benefits of mindfulness and meditation. One of the most renowned researchers, Jon Kabat-Zinn - who introduced MBSR (Mindfulness Based Stress Reduction), established the link between this practice and the feeling of well-being, increased energy and gain in clarity.

Other research[7] shows the extent to which such practices support attention, reinforce the immune system and improve relationships. Don't hesitate: today, rise up and enjoy these "balcony" moments!

How will you feel when you take some distance?

Follow the guide

These steps will help you "go on the balcony", sooth an agitated mind and create more clarity in a few minutes:

- **Sit down comfortably: back straight, shoulders relaxed and hands placed on thighs or knees.**
- **Relax your facial muscles and focus on your breathing. Follow the air entering your nostrils, filling your lungs and exiting through the mouth. Your breathing grounds you in the present.**
- **Imagine the balcony of a theatre. You are the spectator of your own life, the witness of your experiences.**
- **Without judgement but with curiosity, observe your body and energy level.**
- **Listen to your heart and identify the emotions that you are experiencing at this moment.**
- **Still on the balcony, focus your attention on your thoughts. Without judgement, observe what occupies - or preoccupies - your mind.**
- **Finally, remember what matters most to you, the people you love and the values that drive you.**

---

7 R. Davidson et al., "Alterations in Brain and Immune Function Produced by Mindfulness Meditation", Psychosomatic Medicine, 2003. Y. Tang et al., "Short-term meditation training improves attention and self-regulation", PNAS, 2007. CA. Hutcherson et al., "Loving-Kindness Meditation Increases Social Connectedness", Emotion, 2008.

Practice #70 - Schedule 3 time slots to deal with emails

Today, deal with emails during three set time windows instead of reacting instantaneously when they land into your mailbox: 8:30-9:00, 12:00-12:30, 16:30-17:00.

Checking emails whilst reading a report or preparing a presentation affects attention. Research[8] shows that distractions - however minor - can have considerable negative effects. Recovering the original momentum with the same level of concentration can take more than 20 minutes (on average 23 minutes and 15 seconds!). You may believe that you are back to work quickly, but your mind is still processing the content of the message that distracted you.

Why not protect your cognitive resources and stay focused on the current task?

Are you ready to schedule "email time slots" as of today?

Practice #71 - Demonstrate agility

Today, demonstrate agility by operating quick adjustments to adapt to a new context.

Companies no longer use the same working methods as they did five years ago and future mutations will prove quicker and more disruptive still. Change is the new norm and agility has become a fundamental competency: the capacity to quickly adapt to market changes. In other terms: being agile means being prepared,

---

8 G. Mark, "The cost of interrupted work: more speed and more stress", University of California, 2006.

being simultaneously quick and fluid. This means reframing thoughts, adjusting priorities and realigning actions to take advantage of a new possibility or to welcome an unexpected event as an opportunity.

How will you demonstrate agility today?

Practice #72 - Learn something new

Today, decide to learn something new.

Science has demonstrated the amazing plasticity of the brain. Between the ages of 7 and 17, the learning capacity is particularly high; the brain is malleable: connections form and dissolve at extraordinary speed. Beyond that age, the learning speed slows down BUT does not deteriorate. Stress, sleeplessness and lack of exercise are the main causes for the slowdown of the brain. By looking after yourself and committing to intellectually stimulating activities, the brain will help you stay on top of things! Learning something new allows you to live a new experience, expanding your understanding of the world and liberating your potential.

What new thing will you learn today?

What if this were you?

At 55 years of age, Caroline´s fantastic career is almost over. After working for 30 years, Caroline has decided to take an early retirement. Tired of long work trips and longing for more MT (Me Time - check practice #56), she has spent the past six months discovering a new life free of professional constraints. She enjoys the advantages but quickly feels the need for intellectual stimulation, which has always been very important in her life. Her departure from working life

does not quench her thirst for learning. Caroline asks for her friends' advice, browses through on-line training websites and explores the plethora of courses on offer.

She makes a choice and signs up for a few courses that she decides to follow – at her own pace and from home. These new discoveries and the joy of learning give even more meaning to her decision to quit her job. Caroline can now truly enjoy this new stage in her life.

In a continuous learning intent, Caroline stimulates the organ of thought and initiates a virtuous circle, thus creating new neuronal connections that contribute to the efficiency of her brain. She also honours what she feels is important and blossoms in her new life.

Practice #73 - Delegate intelligently

Today, check your projects with the firm intention of delegating some of your workload intelligently. This will allow focusing personal resources on key priorities.

Do you have an endless list of projects? Do you take advantage of the talents around you? Keeping all the work to yourself results in micro-management, accumulation of information and could end in a burnout... and this is true for both working and family life. However, delegating comes easier to some than to others depending largely on self-confidence and trust. Sharing responsibilities - fairly and intelligently - is encouraging to family members and co-workers.

By finding the right balance between the autonomy granted and considerate supervision, you are liberating the potential of those to whom you delegate a project or a task whilst alleviating your workload.

How much are you prepared to share your responsibilities?

Follow the guide

Delegating is an art that needs to be done consciously to be efficient. Consider the following steps:

- **First of all, identify the priorities on which to focus attention and energy.**
- **For each project, list the necessary competencies to successfully reach the objective.**
- **For each person to whom you could delegate a project or a task, evaluate the existing competencies and motivation to take responsibility.**

If the competencies are high but the motivation is weak, think of something that will trigger enthusiasm.

If competencies are insufficient but will is high, envision the support that could equip the person with the required competencies.

If the competencies are insufficient and the will is too weak, look at the facts: the person is not a good candidate to complete the project.

If the competencies and the will are both high, the conditions for a successful delegation are fulfilled.

- Whilst leaving some freedom as to the execution of the tasks, choose specific indicators to follow the project progress and evaluate its accomplishment together.
- Ensure that all intermediate stages are set out to encourage the person in charge and suggest corrective actions if necessary.

Enjoy the free time and focus on your priorities!

Practice #74 - Save time and monotask

Today, focus on one activity at a time and monotask.

Considering the fast pace of work and increased workload, many see multitasking as THE ultimate solution for efficiency. One only needs to look at the number of opened tabs on a computer desktop...

Yet, recent scientific research unequivocally demonstrated that multitasking is a myth. Instead of allowing you to do several things at once, your attention functions sequentially, switching from one task to the other very quickly. Earl Miller, professor of neuroscience at the MIT (Massachusetts Institute of Technology) warns: "Switching from task to task, you think you're actually paying attention to everything around you at the same time. But you're actually not"[9].

An American study published in the Journal of Experimental Psychology[10] estimates that the drop in productivity linked to multitasking can reach 40%. The same study showed that multitasking increases the levels of cortisol and adrenalin (also known as stress hormones).

More worryingly, a study[11] carried out by the University of Sussex (England) confirmed the cerebral nuisances resulting from multitasking. Researchers observed in frequent multi-taskers a drop in the density of grey matter in the area of the brain in charge of empathy and emotional control.

In a connected world where we are constantly on demand, the temptation to switch, scatter and manage all at once is huge. By creating a monotasking habit, you dedicate your energy to execute one task at a time. The quality of your work is higher and your stress level is lower.

Which task will get your full attention now?

---

9 J. Hamilton, "Think you're multitasking? Think again", National Public Radio article, 2008.

10 J. Rubinstein, "Multitasking: switching costs", American Psychological Association, 2001.

11 K. Loh, Dr R. Kanai, "High media multi-tasking is associated with smaller grey-matter density in the anterior cingulate cortex", University of Sussex, Plos One, 2014.

Follow the guide

Face it: your brain is not equipped to multi-task. Even under pressure, follow these 5 tips to concentrate on one thing at a time until it is complete. This will help you save time and energy.

- Choose THE task that deserves your full attention.
- Plan a moment during which you will monotask.
- Eliminate as many distractions as possible! Put your phone away, close your email and if possible, turn off all screens.
- Schedule a micro-break after 40 minutes (check practice #5).
- Execute the task until it is complete.

When you get up and move you are stimulating the oxygenation of your brain, thus supporting your attention.

Monotasking can become a habit. What if you have just too much on your plate? Prioritize and work sequentially rather than simultaneously. You will be more efficient and your mind will be at peace.

Practice #75 - BAM (Breathe, Accept, Move on)

Today, when you feel frustrated about something over which you have no control, try BAM: Breathe/Accept/Move on.

A meeting that didn't go as planned, health issues, disappointing sport results… there are many reasons to mope around and ruminate.

Whilst a deep breath almost immediately leads to a higher state of consciousness, acceptance is the objective recognition of reality. You can choose to disapprove a behaviour or situation, but acceptance avoids suffering.

In the thirties, Protestant theologian Reinhold Niebuhr[12], wrote what would later become known as the "Serenity Prayer" notably used in AA meetings:

"God grant me the serenity

to accept the things I cannot change;

courage to change the things I can;

and wisdom to know the difference."

Letting go liberates energy, which can then be used to learn and progress.

How will BAM help you to progress today?

Practice #76 - Do less, think more

Today, take 20 minutes to think deeply about something specific.

Days are typically structured around the to-do list. Amidst this frenetic busyness, thinking time tends to decrease or disappear. According to results of a 2010 BASEX[13] survey: 58% of those interviewed feel that they only have 15-20 minutes per day to think. 30% indicate not having a single minute to think during the day. This is very worrying in view of today's world issues...

The challenge consists in finding a working method, which is creative and impactful rather than agitated and precipitated.

Who will benefit from your reflection today?

---

12 Karl Paul Reinhold Niebuhr (1892-1971) is a protestant American theologian renowned for his studies on the relations between Christian faith and reality of modern politics and diplomacy.

13 Basex, "Information overload calculation", Basex report, 2010.

Practice #77 - Use the telescope

Today, grab every opportunity you can to look at your choices from a distance.

A hectic schedule and short-term objectives may lead you to lose sight of your long term vision of work. Think about a crew without a captain or clear direction...everybody is busy trying to weather a storm and running left right and centre. The efforts provided are huge but uncoordinated. The crew resists but there is little progress and the risk of exhaustion is near. Many businesses suffer from a lack of direction: long-term vision is stifled by unforeseen circumstances and crises. Even if - or particularly if - times are hard, stick to a long term vision that you will use as a compass to assess the pertinence of your choices.

Whilst recognising the immediate benefits of your actions, it is key to question their long-term impact. Keeping in mind an inspiring vision to ensure that actions remain consistent will alleviate tensions linked to a short-term vision.

How will your long-term vision guide your choices today?

Practice #78 - Keep it simple

Today, keep it simple when sharing an idea or opinion.

A key error consists in mixing up complexity and productivity. Too often, we complicate our messages when simplicity is key for the clarity of the mind. Conciseness and simplicity demand trust and humility. Leonardo Da Vinci used to say, "Simplicity is the ultimate sophistication".

Apple founder and former CEO Steve Jobs also championed simplicity. "That's always been one of my mantras: focus and simplicity. Simple can be harder than complex: You have to work hard to get your thinking clean to make it simple, but it's worth it in the end because when you get there, you can move mountains."

How will simplicity serve you today?

Practice #79 - Say NO

Today, practice saying NO consciously by honouring your priorities.

Saying no is key to personal affirmation. It is not a sign of weakness; it is a component of your professionalism. By being fully aware of the reasons leading you to say no and being guided by your beliefs, there is no room for guilt.

When you respect boundaries, you are giving yourself the means to honour key priorities and to demonstrate assertiveness.

What will you say YES to today?

What if this were you?

Jean has worked as a janitor for fifteen years. He looks after the maintenance of several buildings in his neighbourhood. Devoted and motivated by his job, Jean is intent on being available for all the inhabitants of the buildings for which he cares. Jean is also very involved in his town, his children's school and in a sports club. He is liked for his availability, high-quality work and reliability. At work, at home, with his friends or in his city, everyone knows that they can always rely on Jean.

Professionally and personally, this year is proving very difficult. Jean feels physically exhausted, which prevents him from progressing in his projects. He feels guilty for this drop in productivity.

He confides in a coach, who encourages him to make conscious choices about how he wants to use his energy. This involves saying NO more often to things that don´t match the priorities of the moment. This is a difficult intent for someone willing to contribute actively to the community life and appreciating recognition...

Determined to recover his energy level, Jean decides to test this practice and commits to saying NO at least once a day - whilst creating awareness as to what he says (and often expressing) YES to. The practice proves a lot easier than he thought, and Jean quickly regains a level of energy up to his ambition.

◗ By identifying his priorities, Jean learns to say NO more serenely. When he says NO, he remembers to acknowledge what he says YES to. He thus honours his priorities and reinforces his assertiveness.

Practice #80 - Land twice in a meeting

When you arrive in meetings this week, take a moment to land twice... with your full attention.

By attending one meeting after another, you may very well be physically present, but not mentally. Focusing your attention of sensations of the "here and now" supports presence. Meetings become more constructive and shorter! You could perhaps suggest this method to a colleague? By taking a short moment together to "land twice" - through some silent time, deep breathing or the intent to request the full presence of all the attendees, you are creating an environment conducive to high-quality meetings.

Note that this practice is very useful at home: when you get home in the evening, take a moment to land with your undivided attention, thus becoming truly present for your family.

How about being fully present for the next meeting?

CHAPTER V

SPIRIT IN ACTION

Practice #81 - Demonstrate courage

Today, choose an occasion to demonstrate courage, by making a difficult decision or having a frank conversation, for example. Since the Antiquity and in most civilisations, courage - from "cor", the Latin word for "heart" - is one of the main virtues; it is the opposite of cowardice. Many situations and behaviours require courage: the courage to change, to make a decision, express one's opinion, to commit to something, to love, to give up... Courage means addressing the real issues - often difficult - by making responsible choices. As shown in practice #82, staying faithful to your own values and showing integrity demands courage, which goes hand-in-hand with consistency. Courageous behaviour also instigates trust and gives others an inspiring example. As Nelson Mandela (1918-2013) said: "I learned that courage was not the absence of fear, but the triumph over it." Courage is not innate. Courage is like a muscle that needs training: when you demonstrate courage by going beyond your fears for the right reasons, you train yourself to be courageous in other circumstances too.

How will you demonstrate courage today?

Practice #82 - Be guided by key values

Today, use your own values to guide you when making a meaningful decision and showing integrity. Values illustrate what you consider as essential to arbitrate your choices. Your values are (or should be) your drivers in life. Your values are a compass that indicates the direction to the "true self". When you consider these values in a decision-making process, you show integrity and tackle issues with more trust and clarity. When you are aware of your own values and when they feed on your actions, you are more grounded, life is more fulfilling and your mind is peaceful. You inspire trust and maintain harmonious relationships with others.

What value will you honour today?

Follow the guide

Important choices are much easier to make and results prove more fulfilling when your decisions are assessed using a matrix of well-understood personal values. Here is a 10-step exercise to clarify and foster your own values:

- What do you do when you have a free moment? What are your favourite leisure activities?
- Identify one or more intense moment(s) when your life was particularly fulfilling or poignant (in the positive sense of the term).
- For each answer, ask yourself how it contributes/ed to your life (sleep for instance).
- Go one step beyond: when you were immersed in that dimension, how did it contribute to your life? (For example: relaxation)

- And when you are completely in this dimension, what other essential feelings do you experience? (Inner peace for instance)
- Make a list of keywords and regroup the words/concepts that go together. Identify 3 to 5 main groups (for example: health, family, adventure, freedom, impact, safety, etc.)
- Prioritise the groups. Give a score of 1 to 10 (1 being lowest) reflecting your current level of satisfaction compared with these values (how do you currently experience these values)?

Choose a value that you would like to honour. Think about one action that you are going to take - within the next 2 days - to increase your satisfaction score by 1 point. Are you ready to commit to taking this action to feed one of your key values?

Practice #83 - Make a random act of kindness

Today, seize an occasion to make a random act of kindness. Nurturing kindness is priceless in the professional and personal context alike. Being kind to others is also good for you! The York University (England) published a study[1] where participants were asked to be kind with another individual for 5 to 15 minutes per day for one week. Six months later, participants still felt the benefits of kindness including a higher sense of happiness and reinforced self-esteem. Simple things work best: invite a new neighbour for dinner, get in touch with a distant family member, ask a new colleague for

1 J. Chin, L. Shapira, "Practising Compassion Increases Happiness and Self-Esteem", Journal of Happiness Studies, 2011.

lunch, tell your boss which of his/her qualities you appreciate best, write an uplifting note to a friend in need, etc. Kindness in the work environment does not happen naturally. However, a good atmosphere at work reflects on employee morale, thus indirectly on their commitment and performance. Kindness seems to be equally beneficial for adults and children. In his book on pro-social behaviours[2], German psychologist Hans-Werner Bierhoff demonstrates that children who are kind and attentive to others are not only better appreciated at school but also obtain better marks.

What random act of kindness will you make today?

Practice #84 - Experiment mindfulness around a hot drink

Today, take three minutes to experiment mindfulness around a cup of tea or coffee. Mindfulness is not limited to meditation (check key practice #100). It consists in observing and recognising what happens in your inner self at the present time, regardless of your activity. Since it has been subject to increasing research in neuroscience and enjoys extensive media coverage, mindfulness is no longer reserved to a handful of insiders and is accessible to all, young and old. Sitting in front of a hot drink, you can smell its aromas, feel the heat of the cup held inside your hand, hear the sound of the spoon. You are experiencing mindfulness: being wholly dedicated to what you are feeling here and now.

How does your coffee/tea taste today?

---

2 Bierhoff, "Prosocial Behavior", Psychology Press, 2002.

wroooom
tic tic tit...

What if this were you?

Thomas is a nurse in the Paediatric section of a large hospital. Difficult schedules, intense emotions and a measly salary do not alter his motivation and love for his work. However, he finds it difficult to stop thinking about the suffering that he sees every day, the distress of parents and the helplessness of doctors in certain situations. Reading an article on the benefits of mindfulness, he learns that daily activities can be "mindfully" experienced and can sooth an agitated mind. Why not try the mindfulness experience as he drinks his morning coffee before leaving for the hospital? He enjoys the experience and savours his last minutes during which he can focus on himself and the present moment without any expectation other than simply being there.

Mindfulness is accessible to everyone; it is nothing more than paying attention without judgment in the present moment. By linking it to an everyday activity, such as drinking coffee, Thomas creates a resilient habit. For a few minutes every day, his attention focuses on sensations triggered by this simple activity and he can start his day with a calmer mind.

Practice #85 - Wake up early and "sweeten" your day

Tomorrow, get up 10 minutes earlier than usual and give a sweet start to your day! What are the first minutes of your day usually like? Do you hurry to get dressed? Are you already running around to get ready? Do you feel pressured from the moment you wake up? The way in which you manage your time in the morning influences the way you will spend the rest of your day. "The early bird catches the worm!" and scientific research favours "morningphiles". Waking up at dawn is associated with an optimistic, happy and conscientious temperament[3]. Early risers all agree that the first minutes of their day are a precious gift and they easily spend 30 minutes or more to their morning activity: writing, reading, stretching or meditating. For the others - the night birds - cutting short their nights' sleep is an unrealistic torture. If you are a night bird that gets up as late as humanly possible, remember that, beyond the waking time, your first activities will set the tone for the day.

How sweet will your day be tomorrow?

Practice #86 - Demonstrate compassion

Today, seize as many opportunities as you can to be attentive to others and demonstrate compassion. Compassion comes from the Latin word *benevolens*, which means "meaning someone good". It is the affective disposition of an intent aiming at the good and happiness of others. Showing the people around you that you want them to feel good is a resourceful manner to create a positive atmosphere at home and at work. Moreover, compassion at home underlies healthy and strong relationships. In his book Altruism: the power of compassion (published in 2013, Nil), Mathieu Ricard highlights that we are all able to foster compassion. Daring to thread the path of compassion is the way to a better world and a viable planet for future generations. In a word, compassion is a necessity, not a luxury. Several research demonstrate that compassion at work has many benefits: talent retention, bet-

3 C. Randler, "Proactive people are morning people", Journal of Applied Social Psychology, 2009. R. Biss, "Benefits of rising early", American Psychology Association Journal, 2012

ter relationships and improved health. In 2014, the University of Warwick (England) published a study[4] demonstrating that the productivity of a team that is happy at work increases by 12%. Compassion at work goes beyond colourful offices and a football table in the cafeteria! It is a fundamental work that questions management methods: putting humans back at the core of preoccupations, cultivating civility, taking time to greet co-workers and encourage risk-taking. Increasingly, many companies are on the path of compassion and integrate human and societal factors in the performance evaluation.. Let us hope that this will become a standard in the years to come.

How will you demonstrate compassion today?

Practice #87 - Be humble

Today, cultivate humility. "We shall be content with saying that humility is the modesty of the soul; it is the antidote of pride", said Voltaire (1694-1778) in his 1764 philosophical dictionary where humility is presented as a rare virtue. Are things any different today? Is humility taught, valued, truly appreciated? Often associated to weakness, humility does not get the attention it deserves as a human quality. Yet, are the most inspiring people not the humblest? Humility opposes a distorted vision of oneself, whether it is pride, egocentricity, narcissism or arrogance. Someone humble does not feel inferior to others. In the same way, that same person no longer feels superior; it is a realistic vision of oneself. Humility is an inner attitude that needs to be strengthened. It is not innate but is acquired in time and goes hand in hand with better self-awareness. When coupled with

4 A. Oswald et al., "Happiness and productivity", University of Warwick, 2014.

assertiveness, humility allows appreciating and occupying a fair place in society. Humble people will welcome remarks and criticisms, knowing that it is a fundamental key to evolve and build a trusting relationship. In the same way, humility leads to perceiving failure not as tragedies but as learning experiences. Whilst authoritarian power in the working environment is questioned, a 2015 study published in the Journal of Management Studies[5] indicates that humble leadership is more influential and is associated with higher performance. In some way, it is putting one´s ego at the right place and using it wisely.

Are you ready to feel the power of humility?

Follow the guide

How can we stay humble and avoid the traps of excessive self-criticism or false modesty? These 5 suggestions will help reinforce humility whilst preserving assertiveness:

- Recognise your limitations and fragilities without self-depreciating. By depreciating oneself, you fall into an ego-trap by revealing - erroneously or not - a false image of your capacities.
- Welcome and respect the opinion of others. No one has the monopoly on truth. If they did, we should all have to abide to a unique thought and its corollary, narrow-mindedness. Ask for the opinion of others at home, in a meeting or with friends and keep the door open to dialogue.
- Listen more than you speak. Try to understand before trying to be understood.
- Give yourself and others the right to be wrong. Humble people are not ashamed to bring up their failures or errors,

5 A. Yi et al., "Do humble CEOs matter? An examination of CEO humility and firm outcomes", Journal of Management, 2015.

which help to learn and progress. It creates a climate of trust that encourages initiatives.

- Share success and consider everyone's contribution in any achievement. The greatest professional or personal achievements stem from teamwork. Expressing your gratitude and appreciating others shows humility.

Practice #88 - Make time for what matters most

Today, choose an action that honours what truly matters. You probably know what is "essential" in your life but find it difficult to save time for it. Acting according to the essentials in life requires planning and considering what matters most as a priority! Bronnie Ware, an Australian nurse who worked in palliative care for several years, compiled the The top five regrets of the dying (2011) in a book. In her poignant testimonial, 5 common themes emerge when people speak of their regrets at this crucial moment in their lives.

1. I wish I'd had the courage to live a life being true to myself, not the life others expected of me.
2. I wish I hadn't worked so hard.
3. I wish I'd had the courage to express my feelings.
4. I wish I had stayed in touch with my friends.
5. I wish that I had let myself be happier.

Recurrently remember the essentials in life, act accordingly and you will enjoy a lifetime of harmony with your own values. It is up to you to find the balance between respecting everyday constraints and following your heart. At the end of the journey, when you will look in the rear-view-mirror, the feeling of having lived a consistent life will probably prove a determining factor to having fewer regrets and more serenity.

How will you honour what truly matters today?

Practice #89 - Be joyful

Today, foster a joyful state of mind by valuing a reason to be in joy. In his book on ethics, Dutch philosopher Spinoza (1632-1677) praises joy more than any other quality. He presents it as the conquest of a better relationship to oneself and the world, as an action enlightened by knowledge. The more you know, the more joy grows inside you, making you stronger. Joy is more durable that a passing pleasure and more accessible than happiness; it indicates a feeling of expansion and self-accomplishment. German philosopher Nietzsche (1844-1900) dedicated a large part of his work to joy, which he felt was the remedy to life's pessimism and tragedies. He addresses joy like a fight to accept what cannot be changed, "accepting what is". In his book *La philosophie de la joie*, Swiss philosopher Alexandre Jollien recommends joy as an ethic of life. Positive psychology demonstrates that the brain can be trained to be more joyful. It is not a question of ignoring the truth or pretending that everything is fantastic when it obviously is not, but in the same way as moping around and pondering dark thoughts will make anyone unhappy, choosing to appreciate and anticipate joy is a powerful lever for happiness. When you activate the lever of joy often, you feel lighter, even when your agenda is overbooked.

What will make you joyful today?

What if this were you?

Aged 85, Claudine apprehends everyday life with gratitude and enjoys every day that life grants her. This was not always the case. Life isn't always easy: after a short-lived marriage, Claudine found herself alone at thirty to educate seven children (yes, seven!) with limited financial means, at a time when divorce was seen as a curse. In those days, living was little more than survival for Claudine. Devastated by pain and the fear of tomorrow, she often felt as though she hit rock bottom. Claudine's friends and new encounters re-ignited her enthusiasm to live and experience joy every day. After many years working on herself, reading and meeting other people, Claudine understood the importance of stimulating joy... every day. At 80 years of age, she gets up every morning and feels grateful to be alive. She is attentive to every event - however small - that brings her joy: a blossoming flower, a ray of sun, the visit of a grandchild, an inspiring book, etc. Every day, Claudine experiences joy and, at 80, she is more peaceful that when she was 30.

◗ The combats and challenges of life trigger self-growth, as Claudine personally experienced by welcoming joy as a decision, a life philosophy. Claudine welcomes every new day with gratitude and creates the conditions for happiness. Joy won't wait for years... So from now on, feel inspired to find, appreciate and multiply the instants or occasions that make you joyful, every day.

Practice #90 - Activate the power to care

Today, activate your ability to care for others and give your support to someone you know. As simple as saying "thank you", as bright as a smile, as easy as "are you OK?" care is a choice and power is the base. Biologically, the action of caring for someone stimulates the areas in our brain that are associated with pleasure, the connection to others and trust. In a virtuous circle, this action triggers a rise in serotonin (mood-regulating hormone), dopamine (motivation and pleasure hormone) and oxytocin (compassion and social links hormone). What about those who spend their entire life looking after others? Beyond emotional benefits, volunteers generally enjoy better physical health and tend to be less depressed[6]. However, these benefits are no longer perceived in persons volunteering more than 100 hours per year. Is that the borderline between self-giving and self-forgetfulness?

Who will you take care of today?

Practice #91 - Be kind to yourself

This week, be as kind to yourself as you would to a good friend, and act with compassion, which will lead to more productivity and inner peace. Excessive self-criticism activates the brain's sympathetic system, which raises the level of stress hormones. This can undermine self-confidence and paralyse action. Conversely, self-compassion activates the soothing system; it implies taking your responsibilities to face challenges with a constructive mind. Self-assessment is key in private and working life alike. It invites looking at oneself realistically, without fear, frustration or the need to be perfect at all times. The quality of your inner dialogue is essential for self-criticism to be constructive and beneficial. Being compassionate to others is a good activator for self-compassion: by making the decision to be kind towards others, you will also tend to be kinder to yourself.

Are you ready to be your best friend?

---

6 P.A. Thoits and L.N. Hewitt, "Volunteer work and well-being", Journal of Health and Social Behaviour, 2001

Practice #92 - Tell the truth

This week, tell the truth and say what you really think. Should you really say everything? Is a good lie not better than a hurtful truth? In the short term, it's often easier to lie, but the price to pay can be very high: by cheating people to gain appreciation, you are mixing up kindness with hypocrisy. The question is not so much telling the truth but finding the right way of saying it. You are persuasive and trustworthy when you are honest. As Albert Einstein (1879-1955) said: "Whoever is careless with the truth in small matters cannot be trusted with important matters." Research by Anita E. Kelly[7], professor of psychology at Notre Dame University (Indiana, USA) and her colleague Lijuan Wang even suggest that truth can boost our health. The study also notes that the absence of lies has a positive impact on social relationships. In the professional environment, the culture of constructive feedback is increasingly championed and applies for managers and staff alike. Telling the truth and giving constructive feedback allows for progress whilst lying locks one away in a bubble of delusion.

Will you have the courage to tell the truth today?

Follow the guide

Expressing a harsh truth - to a friend, family member, child or co-worker - often proves a difficult exercise. One needs to find the right moment, the appropriate perspective and suitable words if the person is to understand your intention as a genuine gift. The principles of non-violent communication (language elaborated by Marshall Rosenberg in the seventies) inspired these few suggestions for truth to become a springboard for growth.

7 A. Kelly, "The Science of Honesty", University of Notre-Dame, 2012.

- Have a constructive and positive intention
- Remind the context
- Share your observations
- Express your feelings by using the first person "I"
- Clarify your needs
- Make a clear request

Example:

Intention: I would like to have a frank conversation with a co-worker who is not up to her/his responsibilities and explore together the best manner for her/him to grow.

Context: "You have undertaken your new responsibilities six months ago; your workload has considerably increased and expectations are high".

Observations: "You are making big efforts. However, results are not up to expectations".

Perception: "I am worried and attentive about your future. At the same time, I fear that our project will not come to fruition".

Need: "I need to be sure that we are going in the right direction and identify paths for progress".

Request: "I ask you to think about what will most support you to face the challenges of your new job".

Practice #93 - Cultivate relationships

Today, take some time and energy to cultivate the most important relationships. We are social beings. Our desire for relationships with others is innate and persists throughout our lives; relationships can be the source of the greatest joys and the main reason for suffering. The quality of life at home or in the office depends on how you interact with your family, your neighbours and your colleagues.

A longitudinal study by Harvard University[8], initiated in 1939 explored the factors that make people happy and healthy. For 75 years, several researchers worked consecutively to question the 724 participants on their work, family and health. The conclusion of the study proved both surprising and obvious: the quality of the relationships has the most impact on a feeling of fulfilment, throughout life. Relationships - at work and at home - represent a dynamic aspect of your life that demand care and attention. Even if your colleagues are not by your side in all aspects of your life, they may be the people you see most. Considering the time spent in the office (for many, the time spent with colleagues is well above the time spent at home with one's family), weaving ties based on respect, cooperation and trust is essential.

What relationships will you cultivate today?

Practice #94 - Don't judge

Today, don't judge yourself, others or situations. Education, parents, our circle of friends and the dogmas of society condition us and we often make hasty judgements, which are a means of reassuring oneself and escaping reality. Categorising, labelling, interpreting give a feeling of control but also tend to lock up people or situations in a frozen version. It is difficult to stop judging, criticising and making assumptions. Non-judgement does not only require self-control, but also demands accepting reality as it is, whether you like it or not. Non-judgement is at the heart of major spiritual traditions. According to Buddhism, detachment allows apprehending reality as it is, without being influenced by interpretations.

8 G. Vaillant, "Triumphs of Experience", Harvard University Press, 2012.

In personal coaching, it is a key success factor for a constructive relationship between the coach and the coachee.

What if this were you?

Pierre is attached to his roots: his childhood village. He enjoyed a happy childhood filled with fun and laughter with other children in the village. He studied engineering in a neighbouring town, where he also found his first job. He comes back regularly to his childhood village, where his parents and many friends still live. As his career progresses, his company starts to grow. His expertise is sought and his talent recognised. He accepts a work mission that will take him to Japan for two years. The culture shock is violent. The first weeks spent in Japan confront Pierre to the integration challenge. Pierre finds himself constantly judging - finding his colleagues "too formal", the processes in place "paralysing" and the creativity "tarnished". Pierre then meets other expats who encourage him to understand the Japanese culture better. He quickly realises that his judgements are based on deeply rooted beliefs and habits. By changing perspective and recognising that the behaviours he judges in others are also conditioned by a different culture than his own, he opens up more and no longer judges too quickly. This attitude encourages him to become curious about this fascinating culture and makes his integration with Japanese colleagues much easier.

◗ Pierre experienced the difficulty of silencing his inner judge but also enjoyed the benefits of welcoming the differences. Travel is an extraordinary means of realising that our judgements always result from education, living environment and culture. Silencing your inner judge is an essential step to appreciate difference, which is an enriching factor for personal development.

Practice #95 - Seize the day

Today, appreciate the moment and immerse yourself fully in every experience you live. Carpe diem! This phrase from the Latin verses of Horace (65-8 BC) summarizes a poem[9], where Horace tries to persuade Leuconea to seize the day and enjoy all joys, without worrying about the day or the hour of her death. How can we not worry about the future when we have to manage a thousand things? How can we seize the day while the signals of the world feed our anxiety? Seizing the day is at the origin of numerous ancient wisdoms and at the heart of Buddhism. In the Western world where consumerism and productivity take us hostage in a rat race, seizing the day is almost a luxury. Slowing down to savour every experience is key for your health and well-being.

And how about living the day as a succession of enjoyable moments?

Practice #96 - Be a responsible actor

Today, act mindfully and make responsible choices. In view of the huge challenges of today's world, individual actions may seem pointless. What's the point? I'm not going to change the world. It's not my fault... These thoughts lock you up as a victim. Yet, going from the status of victim to that of responsible person is bringing a positive contribution - however small - to the world. It is an invitation to become active and not passive, as recommended by agro-ecologist and philosopher Pierre Rabhi[10]: "Taking our share is our responsibility in the world.

---

9 Horace, "Leuconoa", Odes, 23 BC.

10 P. Rabhi, *La part du colibri, l'espèce humaine face à son devenir*, Édition de l'Aube, 2009

We are not completely helpless if we decide not to be." Being a responsible actor consists in activating our capacity to choose a response. Any individual commitment takes part in a dynamic collective transformation, such as formulated beautifully by Desmond Tutu[11]: "Do your little bit of good where you are; it's those little bits of good put together that overwhelm the world."

Which responsible action will you initiate today?

11 Nobel Prize winner Desmond Tutu is a South African Anglican cleric and theologian known for his work as an anti-apartheid and human rights activist.

What if this were you?

Pierre Rabhi launched the Association Colibris in 2007. It draws its name from a beautiful and explicit Native American legend. One day, says the legend, there was a huge forest fire. All the animals were terrified and look at the inferno helplessly. The only animal in action was the hummingbird, which used his beak to collect droplets of water to throw on the fire. After a while, the armadillo started showing his annoyance and taunts him: "Hummingbird! Are you insane? You won't put the fire out with a few drops of water!" And the hummingbird answered: "I know, but I do my bit".

◗ What if this hummingbird were you? Do not underestimate your influence and the exemplary role you can play. By being a responsible actor, you are activating the power to choose what you consume, the ideas that you share and the life that you lead. Is the capacity to choose not characteristic to human beings? Now it's your turn to take your responsibilities with joy and consciousness.

Practice #97 - Be open to different opinions

Today, keep your mind open to various opinions. Having an open mind means welcoming different ideas or viewpoints with which you may not agree, with curiosity and kindness.

One-track thinking does not help progress. Limiting oneself to one's own ideas is almost always simplistic. To reach your full potential and develop energising relationships, it is important to keep an open, flexible mind. Others can then serve as examples. An open mind is closely tied to humility. Those who think they know everything never question their ideas and will never learn from others. Remember that curious and open-minded individuals who unlimitedly question the world made the greatest contributions throughout humanity.

How will you welcome different ideas today?

Practice #98 - Plan an activity that proves an optimal experience

Today, create an occasion to enjoy an optimal experience. In positive psychology, the state of optimal experience - also known as "flow state" or "the zone" - is reached when one is completely immersed in an activity stimulating a state of maximum consciousness, full engagement and huge satisfaction in its accomplishment.

Hungarian psychologist Mihaly Czikszentmihalyi (born in 1934) elaborated the concept of flow[12] in 1975 by questioning many individuals from a wide range of backgrounds; they described the best moments in their lives by explaining that they were "as though carried by the flow of a river". The optimal experience often results from a mobilisation and alignment of all your resources: body, heart, mind and spirit. Czikszentmihalyi demonstrated that the happiest people are at their best when they experience a state of maximal consciousness. It is what the runner feels when s/he crosses the finish line, sailors feeling the wind whipping their face, the parent in front of their child's first smile or the emotion felt by the child when riding a 2-wheeled bicycle for the first time. The optimal experience state does not stem from luck (or rarely) but can be provoked. To nurture your happiness and balance, it is important to multiply optimal experiences by transforming some of your everyday activities.

Which activity will lead to an optimal experience today?

---

12 Mihaly Csikszentmihalyi, Flow, the psychology of optimal experiences, Harper & Row, 1990.

Follow the guide

Sought for itself and the immense satisfaction it brings, the optimal experience can take place during your personal leisure (music, sport, reading, food, etc.) or in your work environment (presentations, meetings, discussions, etc.). You can decide to regularly provoke optimal experiences at varying degrees. The three main criteria to enjoy an optimal experience are as follows:

- The purpose is clear;
- The feedback is immediate;
- The needed skills are up to the challenge ahead.

Amongst your regular work or personal activities, choose one that could lead to an optimal experience. Identify the missing element to get there: clarify the objective to reach, develop your skills if you don't feel up to it, transform this activity into a new challenge if you don't feel sufficiently stimulated. Make sure that you are fully engaged and present during the activity. Whilst recognising that some optimal experiences are more intense than others, feel how an activity can be a source of joy when you decide to transform it into an optimal experience!

Practice #99 - Read an inspiring text

Today, set aside some quiet time to read an inspiring text. Reading opens up horizons, inviting us to look at the world differently. Several studies have highlighted the benefits of reading, an effective way to relax and stimulate creativity. A study[13] by the University of Sussex (England)

13 Dr. Lewis, "Reading can help reduce stress", University of Sussex, 2009

demonstrated that 6 minutes' reading are enough to release tensions. Reading broadens your sphere of knowledge, helps understanding, stimulates creative thinking and forges a critical mind. In short, reading is beneficial for everyone, for the relationships with others and for your outlook on the world.

Which reading will inspire you today?

Practice #100 - Meditate

Today, set aside ten minutes to meditate. The term meditation applies to a mental or spiritual practice aiming at producing inner peace and a calm mind. Many think that it consists of "trying to empty one's mind". But this is wrong! When you meditate, you should not try to empty your head, but rather, take an observer's posture and - without judgement - focus your attention on experiencing the present moment: your sensations, emotions and flow of thoughts. Meditating allows for being "awake", fully conscious of oneself. Calm ensues naturally. Molecular biology researcher at the MIT (Massachusetts Institute of Technology) Jon Kabat-Zinn founded the world's first stress reduction clinic based on the precepts of MBSR or Mindfulness Based Stress Reduction. He succeeded in secularising the practice of meditation, making it accessible to as many people as possible. The world of research is excited about the subject and new studies constantly prove the many benefits of meditation on health, concentration, mind clarity, happiness and even on the quality of relationships. An article written at Oxford University and published by The Lancet[14] proves that mindfulness meditation

14 R. Byng, W. Kuyken, "Mindfulness meditation as effective as Big Pharma", The Lancet, 2015.

is as efficient against depression as antidepressants. Richard J. Davidson[15], neuro-psychiatrist and Tania Singer[16], director of the neuroscience department at the Max-Planck Institute (Germany) showed that meditation reinforces the inclination to be kind and to show empathy, which allows looking at (or apprehending) life with more wisdom. You don't need a mat, special clothes or a special room to meditate. You can even do it in bed if you like! It is generally recommended to sit comfortably to sustain your attention. There are hundreds of different meditation techniques. Key practice #69 (Go up on the balcony) offers guidance based on mindfulness meditation. The key to benefitting from this practice is regularity. Many applications including HeadSpace (www.headspace.com) offer guided meditation sessions of varying lengths. After the public health campaigns encouraging to eat healthily and to practice sports, meditation will soon follow!

When is the best time to meditate today?

---

15 R. Davidson et al., "Alterations in brain and immune function produced by mindfulness meditation", Psychosomatic Medicine, 2003.

16 T. Singer, "Loving kindness meditation research", Max Planck Institute, 2015.

CHAPTER VI

IT'S YOUR TURN NOW!

Project yourself one year from now

"If one does not know to which port one is sailing, no wind is favourable" Seneca.

This should remind us how crucial it is to identify the destination before starting off on a journey. For every choice - work, family or personal - forging a vision is like following the lighthouse guiding and steering your choices. In your resilient journey, visualising and describing the resilient person that you will be one year from now is a precious exercise. You don't (yet) have to define the steps required to reach the destination but rather, the result you hope for - the feelings and impact on yourself and the people around you.

Follow the guide

Go to a quiet place and take 15 minutes to do this visualisation exercise. Read through these 10 steps and, projecting yourself one year from now, articulate answers to the questions that will help you - like a jigsaw puzzle - to form the image of the resilient you one year from now.

1) Are you serene when confronted to daily pressures?
2) What is your level of energy?
3) What is your emotional state and capacity for empathy?
4) Do you nurture sustainable relationships with the people around you - at home, with your friends or at work?
5) Can you concentrate and be present despite the endless information flow?
6) Is your mind clear and constructive?
7) Are you able to face challenges with enthusiasm and confidence?
8) How much joy is there in your life?
9) Does your everyday life reflect the importance you give to your own values?
10) Close your eyes visualise your own image and connect to the feelings that will be yours in one year's time, when you are that resilient person.

Choose the right words to describe yourself one year from now and jot down a few lines in a journal.

Where do I start?

To begin, let's clarify what should be avoided. Changing everything too quickly is a losing strategy. For lasting results, small steps matter most. Your routine is what will have the most influence on your general state of mind. Some people reject the idea of a routine and associate it to boredom and monotony. Yet, keeping a minimum routine - that you choose to put in place - is truly beneficial for your work and home life alike. It allows to remain focused and reduces the effects of stress. Although annual vacations are restful, they have very little effect on daily resilience throughout the year. A resilient routine and personal discipline - its corollary - are your most precious tools to truly combine performance and growth.

Follow the guide

- Be conscious of your daily habits. Make a list of what you do every day (or nearly every day) from morning to night.
- Identify your "non-negotiables", i.e., well-rooted habits that serve you and that you want to honour regardless of circumstances.
- In this book, choose the practices that inspire you most and that bring you closest to the vision of yourself one year from now.
- Step by step, transform these desired behaviours into new habits and progressively integrate them to your daily programme.

Many people who have put in place resilient habits confirm the almost immediate benefits, which are often much greater than expected. You can read a few testimonials at the end of this chapter. Very often, the positive impact goes well beyond the scope of the new habit itself. Getting back to physical activity is the perfect example of a habit that affects more areas than just the health/physical dimension. It increases your capacity to manage pressure (stress mastery), stimulates positive emotions and feeds self-confidence (engaging emotions). Furthermore, physical activity reinforces your capacity to concentrate (trains the mind), can nurture the spiritual dimension by reconnecting you to others (if it's a team sport) or to the environment - if you exercise outdoors - as it is also a wonderful way of bonding with Nature. The same applies to many practices recommended in this book that all - generally speaking - reinforce the virtuous dynamics of resilience.

Create a habit

A habit is a behaviour that has become automatic after being repeated several times. Repetition creates the mental association between a situation (the trigger) and the action (behaviour). A key principle of automatism is the absence of intentional thought. You must not think but act automatically. This is the case for everyday habits such as brushing one's teeth or sitting in the same seat at the family table.

How long does it take to form a new habit? A number between 21 and 28 days is often quoted. However, this number is not scientifically proven. Where does the myth come from then?

The 1950's plastic surgeon Maxwell Maltz (1889-1975) observed that his patients needed 21 days to adapt to their new face after surgery. Maltz drew the same conclusion for patients who suffered limb amputation and could still feel their ghost limb for approximately 21 days before adjusting to their new condition. In 1960, Maltz published Psycho-Cybernetics, a book on behavioural changes. The success of the book was phenomenal and the myth of the 21 days was born, without solid scientific proof. Maltz founded his conclusion on the observations of his patients and his own intuition. This "magic" number was appealing as it was short enough to prove inspiring and long enough to be credible. How many days does it take to create a new habit? A scientific answer came in 2009[1].

---

1 Ph. Lally, "How are habits formed: Modelling habit formation in the real world", European Journal of Social Psychology, 2009.

Philippa Lally is a researcher psychologist at the UCL (University College of London) who, assisted by her team, examined the habits of 96 individuals over a 12-week period. Each person chose to create a new habit, such as getting up at 6 am every day, exercising as soon as they got up or drinking 2 glasses of water before eating. Everyone noted whether they had achieved the sought behaviour and how consciously or automatically it was experienced.

To everyone's surprise, it was concluded that it takes on average 2 months (66 days to be precise) to form a new habit. That's almost three times the 21-days myth!

Good news to temper this new finding: the same study demonstrated that regularity is important but not decisive to form a habit. In other words, you don't have to start from scratch when you skip a day. You should however note that a lack of regularity will prevent you from anchoring or automating the habit. The survey did not note any significant difference as to the formation of habits according to gender or age.

Creating a new habit takes more time than we thought and it is useful to persevere. Keeping this in mind, you can adjust your expectations, show some tolerance for any "oversight" and develop strategies to support your motivation until the new habit becomes automatic.

Follow the guide

Creating a new habit is simple, but not necessarily easy. Consider the recommendations below to target the highest probability of success.

- **Choose the right place and time**

Repeat the desired behaviour at the same place and time until it becomes automatic. Deciding to repeat a breathing exercise each day will quickly become a habit if you put in place this same action at the same time and the same place every day. When you will be hurried or distracted, it is very likely that the mind will associate the place and the moment to the breathing exercise. Ultimately, you will not have to think about it, as the automatic response, i.e. the habit, will be activated.

- Make your life easier!

The experiences of others have shown that simple tips can accelerate the introduction of a new behaviour. The objective is to make the task as easy as possible, reducing as much as possible any brain activity that could sabotage the process. If, for example, you want to stretch or do some yoga postures when you wake up, plan to have your yoga mat ready next to your bed. You'll get onto it without thinking. If you have to go and search for it at the back of your wardrobe, the probability of giving up on exercise is high. If you have decided to keep a journal and jot down your thoughts before going to sleep, prepare a notebook and a pencil on your bedside table. Or, if you decide to turn off your screens when you get home in the evenings, have a specific place where you will put your tablet computer and telephone when you cross the doorstep.

- Be conscious of the benefits of your new behaviour

Observing the benefits of your emerging behaviour consists in identifying the reward triggered by your new behaviour, thus strengthening the activated brain circuit. This motivates a jogger who remembers the feeling of well-being after his run, the incentive of the person who meditates and feels calm and inner peace after a session or still, the drive of the individual waking up at the same time every day and feeling in top form. This reward or reinforcement system provides the necessary motivation to stimulate your new behaviour. Being aware and striving for this reward will accelerate the foundation of an automatic habit.

- **Be tolerant AND tenacious**

The above-mentioned study of Philippa Lally reveals discrepancies as to the time necessary to create a new habit. The average 66 days covers important gaps between actions that became automatic after 18 days and others that only became habits after 250 days! Don't be too hard on yourself when your behaviour is long in becoming automatic or when you cannot stick to your commitment. Self-criticism generates additional pressure, which will physiologically trigger a stress response, the opposite of the desired effect.

Persevere and remember that even if it takes a while to anchor a new behaviour, nothing prevents you from enjoying the benefits of your new habit from the first days.

Creating a habit and sticking to it requires discipline. At first, the word may seem suspicious, discouraging and synonymous with constraints, restrictions and self-control. Make no mistake about it, personal discipline will not restrain your freedom! On the contrary, a resilient habit serves your values and is in line with your objective of progressively becoming the resilient person that you want to be a year from now. Your habits aim at nurturing the inner joy as defined by Spinoza[2], for whom joy resides in an action enlightened by knowledge. Spinoza presents true joy as an expansion, an inner-strength to persevere in life.

Thus rooted, your habits will prove a formidable springboard to activate THE RESILIENCE DRIVE.

---

2 Baruch Spinoza (1632-1677) is a Spanish-origin Dutch philosopher whose though had considerable influence on his contemporaries and whose influence persists to this day.

Testimonials

The men and women whose testimonials you will read come from various backgrounds but share one common point: they have all started a process to strengthen their resilience. Most often, they decided to change a daily habit to approach their lives more serenely and with greater impact. In the light of their experience, I hope that you will find a source of motivation to take a first step on the path of resilience.

Christiane Bisanzio – HR Professional – Switzerland

I absolutely fell in love with Resilience due to its compelling science and practicability. I believe that positive change happens only when habits are changed. Resilience enabled me to apply small things, but with rigor and on a daily basis. So I start my day with a minimum of 10 minutes of Yoga. A set of sun salutations and some other postures I feel like to start my day. This practice means that I start the day fresh and with the ability to focus on what is important and what isn't. Another daily practice is the WhatWentWell (WWW). Every evening I spend a few minutes reflecting on the day looking at the positives. I have noticed that I sleep better and can give my dreams a positive spin. In addition, this works really well with my children!

Laurent Jaumotte – Bank & Insurance – Belgium

I noticed that I often lacked presence at work and that my mind wandered in meetings with my co-workers. I realised this after the resilience sessions that I followed together with other members of the executive committee. I decided to put in place a simple habit of finalising whatever I am doing even if this means asking the person to wait, shutting down all other means of communication. I consciously decided to be present and listen by telling others that the meeting can start. This awareness of presence and better listening give me more impact in my exchanges, more personal satisfaction. In turn, I suppose that my interfaces feel more satisfaction since they feel listened to.

Philippe de Korodi – Education – Switzerland

Working for a school is motivating and rewarding but also represents an uncommonly intense professional experience. In addition to modern academic processes, there is the rampant school life and the emotional intensity linked to the parent-child-teacher relationship. Although I was very conscious of my duty to manage priorities and the workload of my colleagues, I had forgotten to manage myself and was not conscious of the advantages of group management. My personal decision to mandate Alexia Michiels from the Resilience Institute to reflect together on our capacity to be efficient professionals in the long term proved fruitful. Thinking resilience, giving oneself the right to look at oneself, to admit one´s limitations and to control one´s workload and many emotions is progress in itself. I also adopted a daily practice that can easily be done three times a day, a sort of mindful mini-break, eyes closed, physically relaxed. Personal detachment allows refocusing energy and releasing the hold of emotions. Moreover, the school´s management committee now breaks its (very long) meetings with gym, dance or yoga exercises. Not only does it help circulate blood and relax the back, but it also helps to relax the work atmosphere.

Xavier Guell - Bank & Insurance - France

When I started in a managerial position, I frequently had to engage in complex situations and difficult conversations. I found that responsibilities come along with presentations, negotiations and other discussions with sometimes difficult interfaces. To manage these new responsibilities, I started practising breathing exercises before engaging in these aspects of my work. Sometimes, I even practice these exercises discreetly during meetings! These breathing exercises allow me to refocus intellectually on the moment and to decrease significantly my level of stress, tension, and even anger. Using this simple exercise, I tackle difficult discussions more serenely; I am more focused and have more impact.

Rosemarie Henning - Engineering - Switzerland

For me, mindfulness meditation is an excellent tool that allows me to face stressful or emotionally draining situations I encounter in my professional and personal life. I focus on my breathing and the feelings in my body and thoughts several times a day. This gently takes me back to the present moment and allows me to develop a more serene state of mind and a more confident, positive and resilient attitude.

Marie-Hélène Massard - Bank & Insurance - Luxembourg

Some days, I have back-to-back short meetings on a variety of different subjects. To be present and active with each person, I take a few deep breaths between each meeting, comfortably seated on a chair. It releases my mind from the previous subject and I feel relaxed to welcome my interface in the best possible conditions.

Thierry Germanier - Education - Switzerland

During a work seminar at the Resilience Institute, I was shown two very simple exercises that have contributed to improve my comfort and efficiency at work: a regular, 20 to 30 seconds deep breathing exercise several times a day followed by two minutes of relaxation exercises for the neck, the back and lower back.

I felt the benefits of these exercises after a few weeks and am now less stressed. Moreover, muscle pain is now a thing of the past and I not only have more energy for work meetings but I am also more available for others throughout the day.

Rosy Khanna - Institutional Banking - USA

I have benefitted greatly from the Resilience Program and especially my instructor, Alexia. The program has helped me reach a level of balance in my life at work and at home. I have adopted a number of practices that I learned in the program, for example breathing deeply 5 times when I wake up in the morning and before I go to bed. In addition, I now have a routine with my waking habits (same time each day), my commitment to exercise and above all to mindfulness in everything I do. I even remember to pat myself on the back with the three W's (what worked well). I find myself going back to my notes from time to time to pick out nuggets that may have been pushed to the back of my mind such as "relaxation is a competence", the importance of "micro-breaks" in an otherwise busy routine, re-centring my "monkey mind" and bouncing out of "thinking traps" and moments when I am too "self-critical". It has been a life changing experience and one I expect to keep in my life going forward!

Vincent Guex - Food Industry - Switzerland

For me, resilience is a state of mind, a drive to take back control of your life in the face of external elements that can have long-term negative impacts.

As far as I'm concerned and very pragmatically, I committed to a couple of sport sessions a week during my lunch break. I use this time to empty my head and the effects are truly beneficial, as I tackle the afternoon more serenely. Generally speaking, I am very conscious of my work time management. After stressful periods, I always find a way to "take things easy" to recharge my batteries and boost my motivation. I have recently started using positive thinking before going to sleep. When I concentrate, I feel its effects with a calmer, uninterrupted sleep.

We need time to create a lasting habit - hence the importance of a commitment to oneself and the will to make an effort for the well- being of everyone: yourself and others.

Elizabeth Davis - Consultant - USA

After I turned 50 I began to notice that I often felt tired and worn down. Many called me a workaholic while I considered myself passionate about my work. Over the course of several months of inquiry, guided meditation, and discussion with family and friends, I had to conclude that I was neglecting my physical being and living almost exclusively in my head, thinking, planning, rehearsing, replaying, but not listening to the warning signals from my body. Learning resilient practices I now have a routine of a morning and evening ritual of loving care. I place my hand on my heart and take three deep tummy breaths to clear my mind and send fresh air through my head and shoulders to my toes. With a long pause for listening, I offer a personal statement of love and care for my body, which allows me to be all that I am, and to express my daily intention to be healthy and strong so that I may live fully into my calling and purpose in this life. Such small gestures of no more than 5 minutes twice a day, I feel a closer connection with how I feel and what I am doing and, most importantly, trust that I can rely on myself to take care of my whole being, not just my thoughts and tasks. I am calmer and more grounded and rest when I know I need it to function at my best.

CONCLUSION

Having read this book, you have started a reflection process and expanded your freedom zone - the freedom to choose. Consciously choosing the actions you undertake, the behaviours that you adopt according to your personal and professional situation within your own constraints and aspirations. This book is not a collection of recipes to find the path to happiness despite life's challenges. It aims at widening perspectives and raising awareness of the impact of your choices. It also creates the conditions that will encourage creativity and self-realisation. When personal discipline serves your deepest ambitions, it becomes your best ally to navigate more serenely through life's many challenges and joys.

In this book, I wanted to combine resilience and enthusiasm. My experience supports my conviction that the competencies that allow to bounce back in adverse situations by mobilising our resources are similar to competencies leading to fulfilment. I am realistic and will not pretend to change the world. I want to trigger the enthusiasm to become the actor of one's own life. Unlike determinism, being responsible entails consciously choosing the response to what life throws at you. Man's search for meaning, a book by Viktor Emil Frankl[3] profoundly inspired me. I specifically remember an excerpt where the author describes how the love and presence of his girlfriend, a young 24-year old fellow prisoner in the concentration camp where he was captive during the Second World War, imposed itself upon him at a time when he didn't know whether or not she was still alive. Through his personal story and the Logotherapy School he created, Frankl insists on the importance of

3 Austrian professor of neurology and psychiatry (b. 1905 d. 1997)

meaning and the spiritual dimension of a person. He wanted to show the readers that life can always be meaningful, even in the most dramatic circumstances. Frankl invites us to say YES to life, notwithstanding its tragic aspects.

Very humbly, I hope that, by nurturing your personal resilience, you will feel ready and prepared to say YES to life day after day and that you will find meaning. May your resilient practices serve your own journey and, indirectly, radiate on others and on the world. If this book has given you some food for thought, a sparkle of enthusiasm or an encouragement to act, I will be overjoyed.

"Freedom is what we do with what is done to us."
Jean-Paul Sartre

ACKNOWLEDGEMENTS

I would like to thank chief editor of Favre, Sophie Rossier, for believing in this project. Her advice, encouragements and professionalism proved crucial in making this book. A special thanks to Aline Lehmann, editor of Favre, for her support and guidance. I am also grateful to Paula Cook for the English translation and her patience with our hours of discussions aiming at finding "the" right word. My warmest thanks go to my dear friend, Ellen Kocher (www.whealthness.ch), for her thorough proofreading. I also thank Jenay Costantini-Loetscher for the illustrations. With her aesthetic trait and sensitivity, she truly embellished the pages of this book.

I would like to express my deepest gratitude to the Resilience Institute. To Dr Sven Hansen for the impetus he has given to my career, for his undying support and his preface; To my associates across Europe - Anne Dufour, Katrien Audenaert, Laurent Levisalles, Thierry Moschetti et Benoit Greindl - for their commitment, collaborative spirit and integrity.

To Joël de Rosnay, who cast his scientific eye on this book and enthusiastically agreed to preface it. Thank you to Frédéric Lenoir for his friendly support. Thank you to all my loyal friends who inspire me with their experiences, courage and creativity. A special thanks to the men and women who agreed to share their testimonials with humility and authenticity.

My boundless gratitude to my parents Baudouin and Françoise Michiels. Your unconditional love built the pedestal of my trust. Thank you to my three sisters, Dominique, Anne-Sylvie and Nathalie. I treasure our family solidarity and mutual affection.

I tenderly thank my husband Benoit Greindl for his support and for every breathing moment. This book would not exist without you. With our four children, you are the essential source of energy and the beating heart of my life.

SHORT BIBLIOGRAPHY

Alexandre Jollien, In praise of weakness, Upper West Side Philosophers, 2017

Alexandre Jollien, *Vivre sans pourquoi*, Points, 2017

Amy Cuddy, *Presence*, Back Bay Books, 2015

Barbara Fredrickson, *Positivity*, Harmony, 2009

B.K.S. Iyengar, *Light on Yoga*, Thorsons, 2001

Christophe André, *Looking at mindfulness*, Blue Rider Press, 2016

Daniel Goleman, *Working with emotional intelligence*, Bantam, 2000

Daniel Goleman, *Social intelligence*, Bantam, 2006

Daniel Goleman, **Richard Boyatzis**, **Annie Mc Kee**, *Primal leadership*, Harvard Business Press, 2002

Daniel Goleman, **Richard J.Davison**, *Altered traits*, Avery, 2017

Deepak Chopra, *Quantum healing* (updated version), Bantam, 2015

Deepak Chopra, *Perfect health*, Three Rivers Press, 2001

Deepak Chopra, **Marie-Odile Hermand**, *The seven spiritual laws of success*, New World Library / Amber Allen Publishing, 1994

Eckhart Tolle, *The power of now*, Namaste Publishing, 2004

Frédéric Lenoir, *La puissance de la joie*, Fayard, 2015

Frédéric Lenoir, *Happiness*: a philosopher´s guide, Melville House, 2016 Fayard, 2009

Frédéric Lenoir, *Le miracle Spinoza*, Fayard, 2017

Geoff Colvin, *Humans are underrated*, Penguin, 2015

Joël de Rosnay, *The symbiotic man*, McGraw-Hill, 2000

Joël de Rosnay, *The macroscope*, Harper & Row, 1979

Joël de Rosnay, *Je cherche à comprendre : les codes cachés de la nature*, Les liens qui libèrent, 2016

Joël de Rosnay, *Surfer la vie*, Les liens qui libèrent, 2012

Jon Kabat-Zinn, *Wherever you go there you are*, Hachette Books, 2005

Martin Seligman, *Learned optimism*, Vintage, 2006

Martin Seligman, *Flourish*, Atria Books, 2012

Matthieu Ricard, **Alexandre Jollien**, **Christophe André**, *In search for wisdom: a monk*, a philosopher and a psychiatrist on what matters most, Sounds true, 2018

Matthieu Ricard, *Altruism*, Black Bay Books, 2016

Mihaly Csikszentmihalyi, *Flow: the psychology of optimal experience*, Harper Perennial Modern Classics, 2008

Mihaly Csikszentmihalyi, *Good Business: leadership, flow and the making of meaning*, Penguin Books, 2004

Willcox, Willcox & Suzuki, *The Okinawa program*, Harmony, 2002

Paul Ekman, **Wallace V. Friesen**, *Unmasking the face: a guide to recognizing emotions from facial expressions*, Malor Books, 2003

Paul Ekman, *Emotions revealed*, Phoenix, 2004

Rael Izacowitz, Karen Clippinger, *Pilates*, Vigot, 2012

Richard Boyatzis, Annie Mc Kee, *Resonant leadership*, Harvard Business Review Press, 2005

Richard J. Davidson, Sharon Begley, *The emotional life of your brain*, Hodder Paperbacks, 2013

Roy F. Baumeister, **John Tierney**, *Willpower*, Markus Haller, 2014

Stuart Taylor, *Assertive Humility: emerging from the ego trap*, Montery Press, 2013

Sven Hansen, *Inside Out: the practice of resilience*, The Resilience Institute, 2015

Viktor Frankl, *Man´s search for meaning*, Pocket Books, 1997